The New Right
v.
The Constitution

The New Right
v.
The Constitution

Stephen Macedo

Library of Congress Cataloging-in-Publication Data

Macedo, Stephen, 1957–
  The New Right v. the Constitution.

  Includes bibliographical references.
  1. United States—Constitutional law—Interpretation
and construction. 2. Conservatism—United States.
I. Title.
KF4550.M22 1986   342.73′029   87-21852
ISBN 0-932790 66-6 (pbk.) 347.30229

Printed in the United States of America

CATO INSTITUTE
224 Second Street SE
Washington, D.C. 20003

For my sister
Carolyn Ann Macedo (1961–1987)

The strength of the Courts of law has always been the greatest security that can be offered to personal independence; but this is more especially the case in democratic ages. Private rights and interests are in constant danger if the judicial power does not grow more extensive and stronger to keep pace with equality of conditions.

—Alexis de Tocqueville
Democracy in America

Contents

Foreword

Stephen Macedo's monograph *The New Right v. the Constitution* contains a number of constitutional ironies. For decades, liberals and conservatives have been divided over the proper approach to constitutional interpretation. The standard liberal view has emphasized the openness of the constitutional text and the need to take changed circumstances into account in construing constitutional provisions. Liberated from the confining notion of Original Intent, judicial activism in support of fundamental values became the centerpiece of the liberal agenda. It culminated in the Supreme Court's most important decision, *Brown* v. *Board of Education*, which ordered the end of de jure segregation in public schools, and, far more controversially, in *Roe* v. *Wade*, which constitutionalized women's right to abortion.

The conservatives have observed a different set of principles. In their view, the Constitution primarily established the rules for the operation of democratic institutions. The structural provisions of the Constitution thus dominate provisions intended to secure individual rights against the government. A presumption of judicial restraint was the result of this fundamental position.

Macedo's essay is yet further evidence that the straightforward dichotomy between left and right, liberal and conservative, is now breaking down. Macedo is to be commended for bringing the libertarian, natural-rights tradition back to constitutional interpretation. He launches a sustained attack on three basic conservative tenets: the doctrine of Original Intent, which holds that the Constitution should be interpreted in accordance with the intentions of the Framers who drafted and ratified it; the assumption that the Constitution organized a system of popular democracy; and the view of judicial restraint that is said to follow from these two positions. For Macedo, the limitations upon popular democracy are as much a part of the Constitution as the institutions of democracy itself. Accordingly, judges cannot indulge the easy presumption that legislation is constitutional unless the contrary is clearly shown. Instead, in each case there has to be a neutral inquiry into how the provisions of a statute square with the language and structure of the Constitution. The invalidation of legislation is not some extraordinary event in the life of a constitutional democracy; it is part of the original design.

The target of Macedo's attack is noted conservative Robert Bork, now on the circuit court for the District of Columbia and frequently mentioned as a possible Reagan candidate for a future vacancy on the Supreme Court. Macedo also criticizes Attorney General Edwin Meese and Assistant Attorney General for Civil Rights Bradford Reynolds.

Macedo is clearly correct in rejecting the idea that the Constitution envisions an unfettered system of popular democracy: the provisions protecting individual rights are entitled to a dignity equal to that of other parts of the Constitution. Although Macedo does not emphasize the point, I am persuaded that the dangers of faction demonstrate the wisdom of entrenching individual rights against the state. The common perception that "special interests" are able to take over the legislature is all too true. The fear of faction in turn raises concerns as to both substance and process. Special-interest legislation, for example, can direct government expenditures to a single group out of general revenues, and it can exempt certain groups from taxation. In each case, the unequal distribution of benefits and burdens is rightly perceived as fundamentally unfair. An elaborate effort to take from A and give to B, such legislation is an appropriate subject for judicial review.*

I would also argue, with Macedo, that one has to be very

---

*My book *Takings: Private Property and the Power of Eminent Domain* discusses the legal principles on which that review of taxation and other forms of government action should be undertaken.

cautious in dealing with the question of "specific intent." Both he and Justice Brennan are correct in insisting that it is fruitless to interpret the general provisions of the Constitution solely with reference to the particular legislative abuses that prompted their passage. Macedo demonstrates anew how circumstances can undermine a theory of specific intent, understood as an effort to seek out the motivations of the Framers. He shows with great vigor the difficulties of ascertaining "the" constitutional intent when all that is available in the record is the inconsistent, ambiguous, and unreflective intentions of the large group of independent persons who participated in drafting or ratifying the Constitution. In this respect, the search for constitutional intent is no simpler than the more routine search for contractual intent in complex multiparty-contract cases.

The jurisprudential concern with intention has another, more useful side, one that should not be discarded along with the vain quest for Original Intent. The invocation of intent can stand for the position that the text of the Constitution has to be the sole source of judicial authority, for if the text cannot constrain unelected judges, then very little else can. Often it is useful to assume that the Constitution means precisely what it says, that the reason the Constitution protects freedom of speech or private property, for example, is that it says so. The text then provides the basis for a sustained analysis of the original provisions, which, as Macedo well understands, need not produce a crabbed or narrow interpretation. This theory of textual intent, moreover, places significant limitations upon the power of the courts to do what they will. Bork, Meese, and Reynolds may be vulnerable insofar as they indicate a dominant role for popular democracy, but they are correct insofar as they rule out the idea of a "living Constitution" that allows judges to disregard the specific text while searching for the contemporary underlying values of constitutional discourse.

Without sound, textually based constitutional interpretation, the shape of the law becomes subject to competing value preferences. Macedo quotes Justice Brennan's well-known George-town speech to the effect that a theory of "specific" intent is an inadequate guide to constitutional interpretation. But Brennan's alternative, his vision of an evolving Constitution, cannot itself withstand scrutiny against a more traditional textual approach. As Macedo points out, Brennan and other liberal thinkers either ignore or downplay property rights firmly grounded in the Constitution's text. Elsewhere in his speech, Brennan insists that the cause of "human dignity" is so powerful that the cruel-and-unusual-punishment provision of the Eighth Amendment should be read as imposing a total and absolute prohibition on the death penalty. This position, however, is flatly inconsistent with the constitutional text. The Fifth Amendment, passed at the same time as the Eighth, expressly states, "No person shall be held to answer for a *capital,* or otherwise infamous crime, unless on a present or indictment of a Grand Jury . . . nor shall any person be subject for the same offense to be twice put in jeopardy of *life* or limb; nor shall he be deprived of *life,* liberty, or property, without due process of law" (emphasis added). The three distinct references to the death penalty rule out the idea that the cruel-and-unusual-punishment clause of the Eighth Amendment bans the death penalty in its entirety. To allow a theory of an evolving constitution to undermine the text is to substitute naked value preferences for law, the abuse traditional conservatives have so long condemned. It is also an exceedingly dangerous practice because once it begins, it cannot be restrained. If one were to argue, for example, that advances in penology and incarceration make the death penalty inappropriate, then someone else could argue that the rapid increase in the crime rate makes the use of torture appropriate, notwithstanding the constitutional prohibition on cruel and unusual punishment.

On the other hand, it is a far harder question whether the cruel-and-unusual-punishment clause imposes any restriction on the invocation of the death penalty in *some* circumstances. That question is troublesome for any theory of interpretation. Constitutions, like well-drafted contracts, limit the domain of permissible choice, but they do not dictate the outcome in all cases. We need, therefore, some sense of the implicit background assumptions against which the Constitution was drafted in order to apply its provisions to the questions that arise over time. It is here that Macedo's libertarian, natural-rights orientation should prove most instructive. Because the Constitution was drafted in the natural-rights, limited-government tradition, modern commentators in that tradition will be among those best able to explicate the principles that make the document so great and enduring a human achievement. Macedo's excellent essay is an important contribution to putting constitutional interpretation back on a sound basis, one capable of sustaining the liberties that are the singular virtue of our republic.

RICHARD A. EPSTEIN

University of Chicago Law School

Preface

I would like to thank the Cato Institute for allowing me to add a substantial amount of new material to the second edition of this monograph. Chapter 6 expands on a talk I gave at Cato's Public Policy Day in Washington, D.C., on May 22, 1987. The Postscript is a revised transcript of my debate with Gary McDowell, former associate director of the Office of Public Affairs at the U.S. Department of Justice, now a resident scholar at the Center for Judicial Studies, and always an able exponent of the New Right's jurisprudence. The original seven chapters are corrected in minor ways, for typographical errors and to take account of recent events.

I hope that this additional material helps advance the argument of the original monograph, but certainly more work needs to be done on the principled alternative to the jurisprudence of the New Right. That project has been importantly furthered by several recent and upcoming publications: *American Constitutional Interpretation* by Walter F. Murphy, James E. Fleming, and William F. Harris, II (Mineola, N.Y.: Foundation Press, 1986); *Takings* by Richard Epstein (Cambridge, Mass.: Harvard University Press, 1986); *The Rhetorical Presidency* by Jeffrey Tulis (Princeton: Princeton University Press, forthcoming); *Theories of Judicial Review* by Sotirios A. Barber (Baltimore: Johns Hopkins University Press, forthcoming); and Randy Barnett's forthcoming collection of essays on the Ninth Amendment. I have benefited greatly from the work and advice of these scholars.

I. Introduction

The rise to power of the New Right is the preeminent political phenomenon of the last decade. Not only have victories been won on tax cuts, domestic-spending cuts, and military-spending increases, but the political agenda itself has shifted in accordance with New Right imperatives. The waxing power of the right is, at the moment, most evident in the White House and the Senate. But whatever happens in the next election, New Right judicial appointees to the federal bench, and those who may yet join Justices Sandra Day O'Connor and Antonin Scalia on the Supreme Court, will influence law and public policy in the United States for decades to come.

In the field of constitutional law, partisans of the New Right advocate a new majoritarianism and a fundamental narrowing of judicial protections for individual rights. The New Right's constitutional vision, if accepted by the nation's courts, would represent a decisive shift of power to legislative majorities and a basic revision of the nature of citizenship in America. A careful examination of the jurisprudence of the New Right is, therefore, in order.

The partisans of the New Right portray their constitutional vision as the culmination of hallowed tradition: they claim to be the ideological heirs of the Founding Fathers and the standard-bearers of the "historical constitution." But the New Right's claim to the Founders' legacy is dubious, its allegiance to the Constitution largely rhetorical, and its stature in relation to the great tradition of American constitutional thought unimpressive. What is striking, in fact, is how far the New Right has departed from the ideas of the Founders, the majestic phrases of the Constitution, and what is best in the American political tradition.

1

Political movements are not monolithic, and no brief work could encompass all the constitutional arguments of everyone associated with the New Right. The discussion in this book, therefore, focuses on a set of claims advanced by prominent New Right scholars and politicians—claims that together constitute the most distinctive and important features of the New Right's jurisprudence. For the sake of simplicity and clarity, the discussion concentrates on the jurisprudence of Judge Robert H. Bork, who has articulated the New Right's most important claims boldly and without inhibition.

It is with good reason that Judge Bork has come to be regarded as the foremost proponent of the constitutional theories of the New Right. As solicitor general, Bork gained national attention when, following the resignation of Attorney General Elliot L. Richardson and Deputy Attorney General William D. Ruckelshaus, he fired Archibald Cox, the special prosecutor in the Watergate affair. President Reagan has recognized Bork's stature by appointing him, along with such fellow conservative law professors as Richard A. Posner and Ralph Winter, to the U.S. Court of Appeals. Bork is quoted approvingly in speeches by Attorney General Edwin Meese III, and he has been scathingly attacked in the pages of the *New York Review of Books* by the foremost constitutional scholar of the left as "Reagan's Justice."[1] And now, as this second edition goes to press, President Reagan has made his long-awaited appointment of Robert Bork to the Supreme Court.

It is not only Bork's notoriety but also his intellectual stature that makes him a formidable figure on the contemporary legal scene. Bork's assault on the active judicial protection of individual rights draws on the strongest and most often used weapons in the conservative armory.

---

[1]See Edwin Meese's addresses before the American Enterprise Institute (September 6, 1985) and the District of Columbia chapter of the Federalist Society Lawyers Division (November 15, 1985), copies of which may be obtained from the U.S. Department of Justice. See also Ronald Dworkin, "Reagan's Justice," *New York Review of Books*, November 8, 1984, pp. 27–31.

First, partisans of the New Right profess a reverence for the "historical constitution" and argue that judges should adhere not simply to the text of the Constitution, but to the text interpreted in light of the specific intentions of its Framers. "It is necessary to establish the proposition," says Bork, "that the framers' intentions with respect to freedoms are the sole legitimate premise from which constitutional analysis may proceed."[2] The New Right is particularly skeptical about the broad rights to privacy and free speech that liberal judges claim to have discovered in the Constitution. Lino Graglia, a likely Reagan administration appointee to the federal bench, denies that the Framers were much concerned with liberty and asserts, "The Constitution's protections of individual rights are not only few but also, when read in historical context, fairly clear and definite."[3]

Second, to circumscribe judicial power, conservatives argue that democracy is the basic constitutional value: "The original Constitution," according to Bork, "was devoted primarily to the mechanisms of democratic choice. . . . The makers of our Constitution . . . provided wide powers to representative assemblies and ruled only a few subjects off limits by the Constitution."[4] Giving majorities the power to pass laws defining how everyone should live is, says Bork, the "major freedom, of our kind of society." And Assistant Attorney General William Bradford Reynolds adds, "It was well understood at the American Founding that all governmental power derived from the people. Nothing other than popular sovereignty could comport . . . with the principles of the Revolution."[5] In construing individual rights broadly,

[2]Robert H. Bork, *Tradition and Morality in Constitutional Law*, Francis Boyer Lectures on Public Policy (Washington: American Enterprise Institute, 1984), p. 10.

[3]Lino Graglia, "How the Constitution Disappeared," *Commentary* (February 1986): 23. See also idem, "Would the Court Get 'Procedural Due Process' Cases Right If It Knew What 'Liberty' Really Means?" *Notre Dame Journal of Law, Ethics and Public Policy* 1 (1985): 813–28. Graglia's position parallels Bork's.

[4]Bork, p. 9.

[5]William Bradford Reynolds, "Reviewing the American Constitutional Heritage," *Harvard Journal of Law and Public Policy* 8 (1985): 226.

say the partisans of the New Right, willful judges usurp matters that are properly legislative.

Third, the New Right claims that "abstract philosophical principles," which are often invoked to support rights claims, should have no authority in politics. For the conservatives, authority resides in the text of the Constitution interpreted in light of the specific historical intentions of the Framers, in democratic principles, and in the "common sense" of the people. Bork, moved by a deep moral skepticism, claims that moral ideas reflect only arbitrary, subjective preferences. Therefore, such "philosophical abstractions" as individual rights should be banished from our political discourse: they dress up and obscure the mere preferences of intellectuals, which deserve no special weight. Political majorities have, according to Bork, the right to define and "suppress" moral harms even if doing so thwarts what some people take to be individual rights or liberty.[6] Similarly, Reynolds derides "the political liberalism of the upper middle class, the university- and professional-school educated . . . the liberalism of a verbal elite . . . out of touch with the mass of Americans today."[7] And for Bork, to require toleration of diversity is to impose moral relativism and to provoke popular "weariness with turmoil and relativism."[8]

Fourth, the New Right asserts that requiring majority respect for minority rights privatizes morality, imposes moral relativism on society, and prevents the formation of a real community. Both Bork and Meese approvingly quote the conservative British jurist Lord Devlin: "What makes a society is a community of ideas, not political ideas alone but also ideas about the way its members should behave and govern their lives."[9]

All four components of the constitutional vision of the New Right, it is argued here, are faulty. References to original inten-

[6]Bork, p. 3.
[7]Reynolds, p. 234.
[8]Bork, p. 8.
[9]Ibid., p. 4; Meese, AEI address, pp. 10–11.

tions do not settle hard constitutional issues. The Constitution does not set up a basically democratic scheme of government but rather a constitutional democracy, a scheme of limited government. Bork's moral skepticism is wholly unconvincing and deeply at odds with the constitutional text and our political traditions: these sources support an active judicial defense of a broad sphere of individual liberties. Liberty and community, finally, are not opposed: a society of free, tolerant individuals is the best form of community, a moral community comporting with America's heritage and the values enshrined in the Constitution. In sum, the New Right invokes "original intentions" in order to evade the only intentions that really count: the purposes embodied in the Constitution itself. The New Right's narrow interpretation of individual rights is supported not by the Constitution but by an ideology of majoritarianism and moral skepticism that is deeply at odds with the Constitution. Against both the New Right and the selective activists of the left, a principled activism in service of individual rights both personal and economic will be urged in these pages. By fusing constitutional interpretation and moral theory, principled activism vindicates the Constitution's authority by establishing its rightness.

II. The Framers of the Constitution v. Judge Bork

Invocation of the intent of the Framers of the Constitution has long been a crucial element in the conservative attack on an active judiciary. Bork is unequivocal: "The framers' intentions with respect to freedoms are the sole legitimate premise from which constitutional analysis may proceed."[10] Activist judges, say conservatives, willfully ignore the intentions of the Framers, insert their own preferences into the Constitution, and in doing so perpetrate "limited coups d'etat."[11]

The invocation of the Framers' intentions has great political appeal. Attorney General Edwin Meese has now made it the centerpiece of the Reagan administration's jurisprudence:

What, then, should a constitutional jurisprudence actually be? It should be a Jurisprudence of Original Intention. . . . This belief in a Jurisprudence of Original Intention . . . reflects a deeply rooted commitment to the idea of democracy. . . . It has been and will continue to be the policy of this administration to press for a Jurisprudence of Original Intention. In the cases we file and those we join as *amicus*, we will endeavor to resurrect the original meaning of constitutional provisions and statutes as the only reliable guide for judgment.[12]

If every phrase in the Constitution were as easy to interpret as

[10]Bork, p. 10.

[11]Robert H. Bork, "Neutral Principles and Some First Amendment Problems," *Indiana Law Journal* 47 (1971): 6.

[12]Edwin Meese III, address before the American Bar Association, July 19, 1985, p. 15. Copies may be obtained from the U.S. Department of Justice.

"neither shall any Person be eligible to that Office [the Presidency] who shall not have attained the Age of thirty five Years," enforcing its provisions would be an almost mechanical process. But even the First Amendment, whose words appear to speak plainly ("Congress shall make no law . . . abridging freedom of speech, or of the press") raises extremely difficult problems of interpretation. The Constitution places a high value, if not the highest value, on democratic accountability, and so we can be confident that part of the purpose of the constitutional guarantee of free speech is to protect free and open debate on political matters. The First Amendment also protects, after all, the rights "to assemble, and to petition the Government for a redress of grievances." When the text of the Constitution is uncertain, help can be sought in the overall structure of the document, the relation between its various parts, or in the nature of the institutions the Constitution establishes. From this more general examination, we can conclude that the First Amendment certainly must protect political speech.

But certain forms of political speech may conflict with government's most basic purposes, such as the maintenance of national security and public order. There are some clear cases: for example, while citizens have a constitutionally protected right to criticize the government (although even that was not always obvious, witness the Alien and Sedition Acts), they do not have a right to publicize the sailing times of troop ships during wartime. But between the easy cases lie many hard ones: Do people have a right to oppose the constitutional order itself? Can people advocate forcible overthrow of the government? Can scholars publish and professors teach doctrines that public authorities consider dangerous to the established order?

Of course, the First Amendment does not specify that only political speech is to be protected; it says simply "speech." But what does "speech" include? Words that offend or libel? Words that some find obscene? Printed material that a majority of the community considers pornographic? Can sleeping in a public park or exotic dancing be forms of symbolic speech? Is corporate advertising a form of speech? In deciding these hard cases, judges have to articulate the basic principles and fundamental values that give substance and specificity to broad constitutional guarantees like the First Amendment.

The many difficult questions raised by the First Amendment are also extremely important. Although particular cases may affect only a handful of people, the principles articulated and applied by the Supreme Court and lower courts help determine the powers of legislative majorities and the rights of minorities. These rights and principles often become part of our political culture, determining in part the sort of regime we live under and the kind of people we become.

While the First Amendment raises a host of difficult issues, it is relatively straightforward compared with the truly majestic generalities that must also be interpreted and applied by judges. Witness the expansive phrasing of the Fourteenth Amendment:

> No State shall make or enforce any law which shall abridge the privileges or immunities of citizens of the United States; nor shall any State deprive any person of life, liberty or property, without due process of law; nor deny to any person within its jurisdiction the equal protection of the laws.

It is no easy matter to decide what these important phrases require, and here the Constitution's structure provides some assistance. Since 1925, the Supreme Court has given substance to the Fourteenth Amendment by incorporating into its general phrases the more specific guarantees contained in the first eight amendments included in the Bill of Rights. The Court has sought, in Justice Cardozo's words, for those principles "of justice so rooted in the traditions and conscience of our people as to be ranked as fundamental."[13] However, referring to other parts of the Constitution may not be sufficient when interpreting a phrase like "due

[13]*Palko* v. *Connecticut*, 302 U.S. 319 (1937).

process of law," which has a historical resonance recalling Runnymede and the Magna Carta.

As hard to interpret as the Fourteenth Amendment is, other parts of the Constitution have been deemed so obscure as to wholly defy judicial interpretation. Consider the Ninth Amendment: "The enumeration in the Constitution of certain rights shall not be construed to deny or disparage others retained by the people." Which other rights do citizens retain under the Constitution? The Ninth Amendment sets a moral question for constitutional interpreters: What rights do people "naturally" have and retain under the Constitution? It is disappointing, but perhaps not surprising, that Supreme Court justices and other constitutional interpreters have typically fled from the hard moral judgments called for by the Ninth Amendment.

How, then, are judges to decide what the Constitution requires in hard cases? They begin with the text itself and seek to understand not only the words but the structure of the document as a whole, the nature of the institutions it sets up, the powers and rights it enumerates, and the principles and purposes implicit in these words, structures, institutions, powers, and rights. Supreme Court justices also have to contend with a 200-year accumulation of thickly textured constitutional case law—interpretations that have helped give substance to the Constitution in previous cases, that have been relied on by lower-court judges, and that may have become part of the public's understanding of our fundamental law. Received authoritative interpretations and practices deserve to be taken seriously. And yet, the Constitution declares itself to be supreme and requires that judges take an oath to support the document itself, rather than past judicial interpretations of it. The Supreme Court, and any other constitutional interpreters, may decide that an established line of interpretation is mistaken.

While text, structure, implicit nature, principle, purpose, and precedent are always helpful guides in constitutional interpretation, they will not suffice for many tough issues. A justice might doubt, for instance, that the Ninth Amendment has been taken seriously enough; he might suspect that people have fundamental rights that are being ignored. But how does he decide what these rights are? Besides using text, structure, and precedent, a justice considering what rights Americans have may turn to our political traditions and to moral philosophy.

Partisans of the New Right seek to constrain the judicial search for constitutional meaning. They insist, as Richard Nixon once did, that Supreme Court justices should be "strict constructionists": they must be prepared to enforce the law as it is and not "twist or bend" it to suit their own personal political convictions.[14] As Bork puts it, "the judge must stick close to the text and the history."[15] These guidelines appear to be innocent enough, but appearances sometimes deceive. By admitting only those rights specifically envisioned by the Framers, the New Right hopes to straitjacket the Constitution's broad protections for liberty by precluding judicial reflection on the Constitution's more general moral purposes. By sticking to strict constructions and historical intentions, judges, say the conservatives, remain within their limited and precarious mandate to review legislative acts in light of the Constitution.

The case for strict constructionism and historical intent is supported by particular notions of democratic authority and individual liberty that are considered later in this book. Here, it is worth considering in some detail the hurdles that must be cleared by the Jurisprudence of Original Intent—hurdles that are sidestepped by Bork and Meese.

First of all, whose intent is to count as original and authoritative? Who were "the Framers," and how are we to make sense of the idea that this large and disparate group had a unified "intent"? Should the intentions of all the delegates to the 1787 constitutional convention in Philadelphia be counted equally, or

---

[14]Richard M. Nixon, as quoted in Ronald Dworkin, *Taking Rights Seriously* (Cambridge: Harvard University Press, 1977), p. 131.

[15]Bork, "Neutral Principles," p. 8.

should the intentions of those who took a leading role in drafting the text count for more? Given the rather spotty records, one would need to rely on the intent of the leading advocates, but clearly, such individuals as Alexander Hamilton and James Madison were proponents of particular and, as it turned out later, different theories of the Constitution.

It was, of course, ratification that gave the Constitution the force of fundamental law, so why should the intentions of the Philadelphia delegates be counted but not the intentions of participants in the state ratifying conventions? Scholarly proponents of Original Intent, like Raoul Berger, seek the intentions of those in Congress who proposed the Fourteenth Amendment, rather than the more elusive but more pertinent intentions of those who secured its ratification in the states.[16]

Should the intentions of those who seem to have misunderstood what was being voted on be discounted? Perhaps, but no such judgment can be made without some independent conception of what the Constitution really means, and that is exactly what the conservatives think we do not and cannot have. In short, simply deciding whose intent counts proves to be quite difficult: it requires an elaborate theory and considerable historical research.

The second problem is to decide what counts as evidence of intent. William Crosskey undertook prodigious research in unpublished correspondence and manuscripts in his quest for the Framers' intent.[17] Raoul Berger, on the other hand, considers only the public, published record of the passing of the Fourteenth Amendment, *The Congressional Globe*, in trying to determine the intent of the Framers of that crucial part of the Constitution. Yet,

[16]See Raoul Berger, *Government by Judiciary: The Transformation of the Fourteenth Amendment* (Cambridge: Harvard University Press, 1977).

[17]See William B. Crosskey, *Politics and the Constitution in the History of the United States*, 2 vols. (Chicago: Chicago University Press, Midway Reprint Series, 1978), vol. 1, pp. 3–14. Here, and in this section generally, the discussion draws upon the excellent Walter F. Murphy, "Constitutional Interpretation: The Art of the Historian, Magician, or Statesman?" *Yale Law Journal* 87 (1978): 1752–71.

records of congressional proceedings may have been edited as is today's *Congressional Record*.

As for the Constitution itself, no official record of the closed proceedings in Philadelphia was ever published, an incomprehensible oversight if it had been expected that future interpreters would be guided by the Framers' intentions. The official record of the convention recorded motions and votes, but not speeches. James Madison's unofficial account of the convention, reconstructed from his notes, was published posthumously in 1840, after everyone who had attended the convention was dead.[18] Meese, however, in defending his Jurisprudence of Original Intent, claims, "The disputes and compromises of the Constitutional Convention were carefully recorded. The minutes of the Convention are a matter of public record."[19]

Even if we were to accept Madison's account of the convention as authoritative and complete, we would still need to confront the fact that public statements often do not reflect actual intentions. How would we distinguish between genuine evidence of intent and the delegates' posturings, rationalizations, and statements for public or scholarly or historical consumption? More basically, just what are intentions in this instance? Are they the Framers' expectations as to how particular provisions would be interpreted, or are they the Framers' hopes?[20] And what of the intentions of those legislators who did not speak?

Let us suppose that the first two hurdles have, against all odds, been cleared: we have decided whose intentions are to count and what is to count as evidence of intent. But after all this labor, we find that the intentions of those involved in the long and arduous process of proposing and ratifying a constitutional amendment

[18]See Winton U. Solberg, *The Federal Convention and the Formation of the Union of American States* (Indianapolis: Bobbs-Merrill Co., 1976), pp. 67–70.

[19]Meese, Federalist Society address, p. 2.

[20]See Ronald Dworkin's important discussion of the problems of Original Intent in "The Forum of Principle," *New York University Law Review* 56 (1981), reprinted in idem, *A Matter of Principle* (Cambridge: Harvard University Press, 1985).

are complex and conflicting. We find that vague and general language cloaks disagreement and constitutes a delegation to future interpreters.

Conservative proponents of the Jurisprudence of Original Intent ignore the crucial distinction between language that is ambiguous, admitting of different but specific meanings, and language that is vague or general. As John Hart Ely argues, "The choice of a general term should, in the absence of contrary evidence, be assumed to have been conscious."[21] Indeed, Meese implies that we should accept the Constitution's general phrases as written and interpret them as such, but he fails to understand that in so doing he undermines his own reliance on specific historical intentions: "Those who framed the Constitution chose their words carefully; they debated at great length the most minute points. The language they chose meant something."[22] To rely on specific but unstated intentions is to ignore the obvious generality and sweep of the language actually chosen. The conservatives would substitute narrow, specific intentions for the broad terms that became fundamental law. The search for specific intentions represents not reverence for, but a misunderstanding of, the project of the Framers.

When it comes to defining constitutionally protected freedoms, conservatives claim that judges should protect only the specific sorts of activities the Framers had in mind. Judges are bound, say the conservatives, to enforce not their best understanding of the general concept chosen by the Framers, but only specific examples of the general concept that some Framers may have had in mind in circumstances very different from our own. However, the Framers of the Constitution were perfectly capable of being specific when they wanted to be: they said, for instance, that the president must "have attained the age of thirty five years," not "the President must be mature." And as Justice

[21]John Hart Ely, *Democracy and Distrust* (Cambridge: Harvard University Press, 1981), pp. 198–99.

[22]Meese, ABA address, p. 16.

14

Frankfurter pointed out in *Adamson* v. *California,* what was voted on at each stage was the proposed language or amendment, not the speeches.[23] Surely there is no reason to suppose, as do the conservatives, that judges are obliged to read the Framers' sweeping phrases narrowly, in light of specific unstated intentions, given that the Framers could have used more specific phrases but chose not to.

The Fourteenth Amendment, for instance, requires that no state shall "deny to any person within its jurisdiction the equal protection of the laws." Should judges be confined to the specific kinds of unequal protection that the "framers" of that amendment might have had in mind? That is, if many of those responsible for the Fourteenth Amendment expected, foresaw, or hoped that it would prohibit racial discrimination in common law but not other forms of invidious discrimination, are judges bound by that concrete, unstated, "intention" to allow all other forms of discrimination, as Bork has claimed?[24] Judges could, instead, seek and apply the morally best understanding of the principles and values that give substance to the sweeping phrase "the equal protection of the laws." Judges seeking the morally best meaning would not engage in historical research designed to "resurrect" the intentions of persons long dead, as the New Right would have us do. Rather, they would seek the meaning that makes equal protection the most worthy value or goal consistent with the other values and goals in the Constitution.

There are many reasons for preferring the latter alternative. Constitutional principles must be applied to circumstances the Framers never envisioned. Even when institutions persist, the passage of time may alter their status in society; public schooling is a good example of that. Further, it may be that particular Framers, at the concrete level, inadequately understood what "the equal protection of the laws" actually requires. The suprem-

[23]332 U.S. 46 (1947).
[24]Bork, "Neutral Principles," p. 14.

15

acy of the Constitution as written, general sweeping phrases and all, may require specific judicial measures that the Framers of particular clauses did not contemplate.[25] Finally, the best reason for even acknowledging the supremacy of the Constitution is the document's conformity with our best understanding of justice. By engaging in moral reflection rather than historical research to complete the meaning of the Constitution's difficult passages, judges help justify and vindicate the Constitution's moral supremacy, help to realize the Constitution's moral aspirations, and help to ensure that we will be governed by more than the will and preferences of the most powerful.

It is with good reason that constitutional scholar Walter F. Murphy argues, "The difficulties that confront any painstakingly thorough and intellectually scrupulous researcher who tries to establish legislative intent are typically insuperable."[26] At the very least, it would take an extremely elaborate theory, a series of difficult judgments, and a wealth of historical research to hack through the great tangle of problems surrounding the Jurisprudence of Original Intent. What began as a flight from hard judgments, therefore, ends in a series of nearly impossible judgments and insuperable obstacles.

The infirmities of the Jurisprudence of Original Intent appear to be fatal. Yet, there is one final disability that would alone prove fatal even to a theory healthy in other respects. Raoul Berger, whose *Government by Judiciary* indicts judicial activism in the name of Original Intent, asserts what other conservatives, like Bork, simply assume: that the Constitution "was written against a background of interpretive presuppositions" and, in particular, that the Framers intended future interpreters to carry out their "orig-

---

[25]See Dworkin's important claim that the Framers should be understood as having enacted general concepts into law, such as "equal protection," but not specific conceptions of what are to count as concrete instances of those concepts, in *Taking Rights Seriously*, pp. 134–36.

[26]Murphy, p. 1761.

16

inal" intentions.[27] If the conservatives are wrong about this particular intention, which we might call the original "interpretive intent," then the Jurisprudence of Original Intent self-destructs. If the Framers themselves did not intend constitutional interpreters to be guided by their specific intentions, then, if only to carry out the original intent, we would have to give up historical research and think about the Constitution for ourselves.

Unfortunately for the New Right, the Framers of the Constitution did reject reliance on historical intentions. The "modern resort to the 'intent of the framers' can gain no support from the assertion that such was the framers' expectation, for the framers themselves did not believe such an interpretive strategy to be appropriate," writes H. Jefferson Powell in his painstaking and impressive study of the historical record. He concludes that "there is no indication that they [the Philadelphia Framers] expected or intended future interpreters to resort to any extra-constitutional intentions revealed in the convention's secretly conducted debates."[28]

So how did the Founders expect the Constitution to be interpreted? There was no original consensus; rather, there were two different views on the subject. Many Americans of the revolutionary period, influenced by the Protestant idea that the truth of scripture or law resides in the common understanding of plain words, were suspicious of any sort of interpretation at all. Others embraced the rich interpretive tradition of the English common law, in which time-honored techniques for interpreting statutes, wills, and contracts were considered an authoritative part of the law itself.

Most of the Framers of the Constitution were, of course, lawyers. When faced with the task of interpreting ambiguous statutes, colonial lawyers and judges did not look to legislative history, as the modern proponents of Original Intent would have

[27]Berger, pp. 365–66, quoted in H. Jefferson Powell, "The Original Understanding of Original Intent," *Harvard Law Review* 98 (1985): 886.

[28]Powell, p. 903.

17

us do. Legal practice during that period specified that judges might look to an ambiguous act's preamble to determine its apparent end or purpose, as well as to its relation to previous acts and other legal precedents, but not to legislative history or to evidence of the subjective purposes of legislators.[29]

During the debates in the states over the ratification of the Constitution, the Framers had ample opportunity to affirm the controlling authority of their intentions, if they had so wished. But to the contrary, James Madison and Alexander Hamilton, who were most prominent in framing and securing the ratification of the Constitution, positively opposed reliance on the intentions of the Framers. They stressed that fallibility and tentativeness were inescapable features of human expression. Constitutional meaning would have to be elucidated and extended by judges in the course of adjudication through reasoned, legal deliberation, not by historical research. As Hamilton put it, "The rules of legal interpretation are rules of common sense, adopted by the courts in the construction of the laws. . . . In relation to such a subject [a constitution], the natural and obvious sense of its provisions, apart from any technical rules, is the true criterion of construction."[30]

Madison emphasized that the judiciary would play a necessary part in fleshing out the meaning of the law of the land, which included the Constitution:

All new laws, though penned with the greatest technical skill, and passed on the fullest and most mature deliberation, are considered as more or less obscure and equivocal, until their meaning be liquidated and ascertained by a series of particular discussions and adjudications.[31]

Some years after the ratification of the Constitution, when debat-

---

[29]Ibid., pp. 896–98.
[30]Alexander Hamilton, *Federalist*, no. 83.
[31]James Madison, *Federalist*, no. 37.

ing the constitutionality of the national bank bill, Hamilton explicitly rejected the relevance of historical evidence of the Framers' intentions:

Whatever may have been the intention of the framers of a constitution, or of a law, that intention is to be sought for in the instrument itself, according to the usual and established rules of construction. Nothing is more common than for laws to express and effect, more or less than was intended.[32]

If the ideas of the Founders at the time they drafted and passed the Constitution positively oppose the Jurisprudence of Original Intent, some slightly later ideas seem, at first, more congenial to it.

The Republican theory of the Constitution, as developed and promoted by Thomas Jefferson and James Madison, secured national consensus 10 years into the life of the republic, a consensus that lasted for a quarter of a century.[33] The Republicans in the early 19th century, like Bork and the New Right generally today, were deeply suspicious of the "wiles of construction," or what they perceived as the tendency to distort the meaning of the Constitution in interpreting it. Like Bork, the Republicans saw constitutional interpretation as a search for the Constitution's underlying and original intent.[34] On its surface, therefore, the Republican theory of the Constitution seems to be a precursor of the Jurisprudence of Original Intent.

But modern conservative intentionalism is not supported by the Republican theory of the Constitution. Republican strict constructionism derived from an understanding of the Constitution as a compact between the states, which retained their sovereignty. Strict constructionism was justified, for the Republicans,

---

[32]Alexander Hamilton, "Opinion on the Constitutionality of an Act to Establish a Bank" (1791), reprinted in *Papers of Alexander Hamilton*, ed. H. Syrett (1965), vol. 8, p. 111, quoted in Powell, p. 915.

[33]Powell, p. 887.

[34]Ibid., p. 927.

by their conviction that sovereign states could not be presumed to have given up more of their powers than they explicitly specified in the Constitution. Thus, the Republicans were mainly concerned about interpreting the federal government's powers narrowly. In contrast, Bork seeks to read federal powers broadly and to read reservations on those powers, including individual rights, narrowly.

Indeed, the Republican theory of the Constitution was developed in direct opposition to nationalists, like Hamilton, who interpreted federal powers broadly. According to the Republican-inspired Virginia and Kentucky Resolutions of 1798 drafted by Madison and Jefferson, the states retained the right to review federal interpretations of the Constitution and to reject those they disagreed with.

Republican strict constructionism depended basically on the assumption that the states retained their sovereignty as parties to a constitutional compact. Bork's argument for strict construction, however, rests on the wholly different assumption that the Constitution gains its authority from the will of a sovereign national majority, which cannot be supposed to have ceded more rights to minorities than were expressly granted. Nothing could be further from the minds of Jefferson and Madison than Bork's claim that the Constitution establishes a national democracy of broad powers with few reservations on these powers. The legal positivism that undergirds Bork's position, the idea that the Constitution is authoritative because of its source in popular will, is deeply at odds with the founding generation's belief that principles of justice and natural rights are morally binding on any act of will. The strict constructionism of Bork and other present-day conservatives is clearly at odds with the ideas of the Founding Fathers.

Some conservatives do argue for a return to the old Republican "states' rights" conception of the Constitution. In fact, many conservatives make more of federalism than does Robert Bork. Meese, for example, approvingly cites Justice Rehnquist's opinion in *National League of Cities* v. *Usery*,[35] in which Rehnquist flirts with the states'-rights view by speaking of "the states in their capacities as sovereign governments" and refers to states as "coordinate elements in the system established by the framers."[36] Other conservatives contend, more reasonably, that the federal government has assumed powers that properly belong to the states, especially certain "police powers," powers to regulate health and safety, powers not related to commerce and national defense, and powers not grounded by any reasonable construction in the Constitution's enumeration of Congress's powers.[37]

It is one thing to argue that the federal government has assumed powers reserved to the states, making a mockery of both federalism and a government of enumerated powers. It is quite another thing, and far more difficult, to maintain that the federal government has overstepped its bounds in defending constitutional rights against the states. The scope of legitimate national powers may be more limited than the powers actually accrued by the federal government, but nothing follows from this claim as to the propriety of the Supreme Court's protection of a broad sphere of national rights. The Thirteenth, Fourteenth, and Fifteenth amendments—adopted after the Civil War—decisively shift to the national government the responsibility for protecting a broad sphere of individual rights against the states.

The old Republican theory, which depicts the Constitution as a compact among sovereign states, and the modern conservative idea, which depicts America as essentially a majoritarian democracy, have one important attribute in common: both are based on implausible conceptions of the fundamental nature of the republic. The Republican claim that the Constitution is basically a com-

---

[35]426 U.S. 833 (1976).

[36]Meese, AEI address, p. 3; idem, ABA address, pp. 6–7.

[37]See chapter 3 below. See also Sotirios Barber's important claim that congressional powers have been used pretextually as a substitute for an adequate theory of constitutional ends, given in idem, *On What the Constitution Means* (Baltimore: Johns Hopkins Press, 1984), especially pp. 101–6.

21

pact among the states is undermined by the fact that the Constitution emanates from and operates directly on the people of the whole nation. "We, the people of the United States," as the preamble indicates, and not the states, ordained and established the Constitution as fundamental law.

Proponents of the modern Jurisprudence of Original Intent, on the other hand, ignore the fact that the Constitution established, and was meant to establish, not a majoritarian democracy but a liberal, or constitutional, democracy. The legitimacy of the national government does rest on the consent of the governed, but not on that alone. Although our scheme of government utilizes some forms of democratic accountability, it remains a system of enumerated or limited powers and broad rights. In short, the Constitution expresses a certain measure of confidence in, but also no small measure of distrust of, democratic government. For the people who drafted and ratified the Constitution, legitimate government depended not only on the document's origin in popular consent, but also on its conformity with certain principles of justice and "unalienable Rights," which were held to be "natural" or of higher moral standing than the will of any majority.

The modern Jurisprudence of Original Intent, therefore, cannot gain support from what is only a superficial similarity to the old Republican theory of the Constitution. Consequently, there is no reason to think that the Founders intended future interpreters to be guided by the Founders' own specific intentions rather than by the general purposes set out in the Constitution itself. The Constitution declares itself to be supreme, and the preamble lays out its objects and purposes in broad terms, including "Justice" and "the Blessings of Liberty for ourselves and our Posterity." The very language of the Constitution suggests that the Framers, as intelligent statesmen, recognized that the Constitution is not a contract or a statute but a majestic charter for government, intended to govern for ages to come and to apply to both unforeseen and unforeseeable circumstances. The notion that specific but unstated intentions ought to supplant the interpreter's best

22

understanding of the general words and structure of the document represents a devaluation of the status of the document itself. It is in light of the aspiration to justice and liberty, and the other objects and ends stated and implied in the Constitution, that the founding document and its problematic passages should be interpreted. By misunderstanding the purpose of the generation that resorted to constitutionalism, the _____ dence of Original Intent have pla _____ destruction.

What accounts for the allure of Intent? What has led the New Righ with difficulties and so patently Constitution? For judges seeking ments of political morality, reso__ __ ___ appears, at first, to be an avenue of escape. And for those seeking to constrain the discretion and political influence of judges, Original Intent appears to be a useful straitjacket. Original Intent, however, can be neither an escape nor a straitjacket, for there is no simple canonical intent locked in the historical record waiting to be uncovered and deferred to. Nor can conscientious interpreters avoid making difficult judgments, for the Constitution itself will not allow it. Judges who wish to live up to their oath to support the Constitution cannot avoid the difficult political judgments with which the founding document confronts them. And those who invoke, against a robust judiciary, the founding document and the intent of its Framers have understood neither.

In any case, the conservative invocation of Original Intent has less to do with reverence for the ideas of the Founders than with a political preference for majoritarian power over individual rights and liberty. The Jurisprudence of Original Intent would render constitutionalism a mere mask, concealing without directing or constraining the sovereign power of majorities. Underlying Bork's version of the Constitution is a majoritarian impulse that, far from being in accord with the intentions of the Framers, is deeply at odds both with the text and structure of the Constitution and the project of constitutionalism itself.

III. The Majoritarian Myth

Despite the great popularity of the argument for Original Intent, it is a singularly problematic and unpromising way to interpret the Constitution. The real basis of the New Right's jurisprudence is not reverence for historical or original intentions anyway, as is evident from the fact that the conservatives are selective rather than consistent in their invocaservatives were really interes tions, they would not simply a intentions with respect to free ise" for "constitutional analys scientious proponents of Origi freedoms in light of specific powers.

What the New Right position really comes down to is the Jurisprudence of Selective Intent: judges are referred to original intentions only when the process serves a deeper political commitment—that of construing government powers and the powers of majorities broadly and individual rights narrowly. This preference for political power over individual rights controls the conservatives' use of the idea of Original Intent and thereby forms the real basis of their theory of the Constitution. In fact, the New Right's commitment to majoritarianism and government power is deeply opposed to the only intentions that really count, namely, those embodied by the Framers in the text of the Constitution.

Innumerable analyses of the Constitution begin with the assumption that America is basically a democratic polity. As Alexander Bickel put it, "Judicial review is a deviant institution in the

[38]Bork, *Tradition*, p. 10.

American democracy."[39] Judges are unelected and are responsible to no constituency, and their power is most controversial when the courts review the acts of elected legislators for conformity with the Constitution. Given the assumption that America is basically a majoritarian democratic polity, judicial review stands out as an anomaly, and the imposition of limits on the review power of judges appears as an imperative. And so Justice Antonin Scalia, a Reagan appointee to the Supreme Court, advocates a "restricted view of the Court's role in a democratic society."[40]

The New Right's majoritarian convictions are straightforward, though sometimes couched in the language of liberty. Thus, Bork quotes the English writer G. K. Chesterton:

"What is the good of telling a community that it has every liberty except the liberty to make laws? The liberty to make laws is what constitutes a free people." The makers of our Constitution thought so too, for they provided wide powers to representative assemblies and ruled only a few subjects off limits by the Constitution.[41]

Bork depicts judicial deference to legislatures as an avoidance of value choice:

The choice of "fundamental values" by the Court cannot be justified. Where constitutional materials do not clearly specify the value to be preferred, there is no principled way to prefer any claimed human value to any other. The judge must stick close to the text and history, and their fair implications, and not construct any new rights.[42]

---

[39]Alexander Bickel, *The Least Dangerous Branch* (Indianapolis: Bobbs-Merrill Co., 1962), p. 18.

[40]Antonin Scalia, "Economic Affairs as Human Affairs," *Cato Journal* 4, no. 3 (1985): 707.

[41]Bork, *Tradition*, p. 9.

[42]Bork, "Neutral Principles," p. 8. On Bork's opposition to the "method of moral philosophy," see also idem, "Commentary: The Impossibility of Finding Welfare Rights in the Constitution," *Washington University Law Quarterly* (1979): 695–97.

Judicial deference, however, is not an avoidance of choice. Rather, it is a choice of majority power over individual liberty. This choice of political values is as "fundamental" and important as any choice can be, and it needs to be defended or abandoned, not hidden under the guise of skepticism, deference, and neutrality.

The selective invocation of Original Intent hides a decided political bias:

> A position that upholds constitutional claims only if they were within the specific contemplation of the Framers in effect establishes a presumption of resolving textual ambiguities against the claims of constitutional right. This is a choice no less political than any other; it expresses antipathy to the claims of the minority against the majority.[43]

Conservative strict constructionists, like Bork, argue in effect that judges should enforce only explicit rights, rights plainly stated in the Constitution's text or very clearly implied in it. Legislators, on the other hand, may do anything that is not plainly forbidden by the Constitution's text and its clear implications. This stark divergence of standards can be justified only by a strong assumption that the overall purpose or point of the Constitution is to empower majoritarian institutions.

The democratic rendering of the Constitution is a crucial underpinning of the selective invocation of Original Intent and of the New Right's attack on the judiciary. But the New Right's strategy for defining individual rights narrowly and government powers broadly rests on a nonexistent foundation: the Constitution is not basically a simple democratic document.

The Philadelphia constitutional convention took place under the shadow of chaos and instability in the states, which the Framers attributed to excessive democracy in the state constitutions

---

[43]William J. Brennan, speech at Georgetown University, October 12, 1985; reprinted in *New York Times*, October 13, 1985, p. 36. Brennan's own reading of the Constitution is, however, no less partisan and selective than that of the New Right.

under the Articles of Confederation.[44] In the eleven years between the signing of the Declaration of Independence and the Philadelphia convention, those who would frame the Constitution learned that making government accountable to the people is not sufficient to secure either order or the protection of liberty and rights.

Direct democracy and majoritarianism were decisively rejected by the Framers, and the system of government established by the Constitution embodies this rejection.[45] Senators were originally chosen by state legislators, and it was only in 1913, with the passage of the Seventeenth Amendment, that they became popularly elected; even so, each state continues to have two senators regardless of population. State legislatures were originally given the power to choose presidential electors, and the less-populous states continue to be overrepresented in the electoral college. Staggered elections, long terms for senators and the president, the system of separated powers, and the embrace by one national government of a large or "extended" republic were all designed by the Framers to make it difficult for a national majority to gain effective control of the government. It was thereby hoped that ample room would be left for deliberation, statesmanship, and the rule of justice. On the "input" or process side, therefore, democracy is tempered and compromised by many checks and balances, including the power of the courts.

As for the courts, it is sometimes argued that those who have libertarian political sentiments should press these sentiments in the political arena along with everyone else. For proponents of rights who lose in the political process to then invoke the power of courts is as illegitimate, as Bork puts it, as invoking the power of the joint chiefs of staff; in either case, it amounts to the perpetration of "limited coups d'etat."[46] The courts have a narrow

---

[44]See Gordon Wood, *The Creation of the American Republic: 1776–1787* (New York: W. W. Norton & Company, 1969).

[45]See the *Federalist*, especially no. 10 and no. 49.

[46]Bork, "Neutral Principles," p. 6.

role, limited to enforcing the specific prohibitions of the Constitution along the lines suggested by the concrete historical intentions of the Founders. Here again, these prescriptions are supported by the implicit idea that the Court's power is somehow anomalous or in need of being circumscribed in a democratic polity.

Nevertheless, it is hard to find any warrant for this presumption against the courts in the Constitution itself. The founding document extends the judicial power "to all Cases, in Law and Equity, arising under this Constitution."[47] Judges take an oath to support the Constitution, and in declaring itself supreme, the Constitution then adds that judges should take special notice: "This Constitution, and the Laws of the United States which shall be made in pursuance thereof . . . shall be the supreme Law of the Land; and the judges in every State shall be bound thereby."[48]

In the first Congress, James Madison proposed and led the passage of the Bill of Rights, explaining that once passed and "incorporated into the Constitution, independent tribunals of justice will consider themselves in a peculiar manner the guardians of those rights." The courts, Madison continued, will be an "impenetrable bulwark against every assumption of power in the legislative or executive" branches and "be naturally led to resist every encroachment upon rights expressly stipulated for in the Constitution by the declaration of rights."[49]

The *Federalist*, no. 78, was Hamilton's extended defense of an independent, active judiciary. He defined limited government as one that protects individual rights through the courts even against "legislative invasions . . . instigated by the major voice of the community." Those who doubt that the Framers intended the

<hr>

[47]U.S. Constitution, Article III, sec. 2.

[48]Ibid., Article VI.

[49]James Madison, as quoted in Robert Rutland, "How the Constitution Secures Rights: A Look at the Seminal Years," in *How Does the Constitution Secure Rights?* ed. Robert Goldwin and William Schambra (Washington: American Enterprise Institute, 1985).

judiciary to play an active role in preserving limited government and individual rights even against popular majorities should pay heed to Hamilton's public declaration:

> The courts were designed to be an intermediate body between the people and the legislature in order, among other things, to keep the latter within the limits of their assigned authority. The interpretation of the laws is the proper and peculiar province of the courts. A constitution is, in fact, and must be regarded by judges as, a fundamental law. . . . [T]he constitution ought to be preferred to the statute. . . . This independence of judges is equally requisite to guard the constitution and rights of individuals from the effects of those ill humors which the arts of designing men, or the influence of particular conjunctures, sometimes disseminate among the people themselves . . . to occasion dangerous innovations in the government, and serious oppressions of the minor party in the community. . . . [I]t would require an uncommon portion of fortitude in the judges to do their duty as faithful guardians of the Constitution, where legislative invasions of it had been instigated by the major voice of the community.[50]

Thus, Hamilton defended the "permanent tenure of judicial offices" so as to make the courts "bulwarks of a limited constitution against legislative encroachments."

The Framers of the Constitution, therefore, took pains to check popular will and not simply to empower it because they agreed with Madison that "the invasion of private rights is chiefly to be apprehended, not from acts of Government contrary to the sense of its constituents, but from acts in which the Government is the mere instrument of the major number of constituents."[51]

So much for the claim that the Constitution establishes simple,

[50]Alexander Hamilton, *Federalist*, no. 78.

[51]James Madison, letter to Thomas Jefferson (1788), quoted in Walter Murphy, "The Art of Constitutional Interpretation," in *Essays on the Constitution of the United States*, ed. M. Judd Harmon (Port Washington, N.Y.: Kennikat, 1978), pp. 130–59.

democratic processes. The Constitution also imposes a number of substantive limitations on the ends the federal government may pursue. The Constitution explicitly denies Congress the power to suspend habeas corpus in peacetime, to pass bills of attainder, to pass ex post facto laws, or undertake certain other actions.[52] It also explicitly denies to the states the power to conduct their own foreign policies, grant titles of nobility, emit bills of credit, make paper money legal tender, pass bills of attainder and ex post facto laws, or impair the obligation of contracts.[53]

The Constitution's specific prohibitions may seem rather thin; indeed, one of the chief complaints of those who opposed ratification of the Constitution was the absence of a bill of rights limiting the power of the national government in the name of fundamental rights and liberties. This absence, however, was not the consequence of any skepticism on the part of the Framers about the existence of broad natural rights. There was probably nothing in politics that the founding generation was more certain of than the existence of natural rights.

As Hamilton explained in the *Federalist*, the enumeration of rights in a Constitution could, paradoxically, be harmful to rights themselves. The Founders distrusted the "aphorisms" that tended to be embodied in bills of rights. More importantly, they positively opposed the natural implication of an enumeration of rights; to specify the rights to be protected against oppressive majorities might imply, wrongly, that these rights were exceptions to a general grant of government powers.[54]

A government of enumerated powers need not specify the rights to be protected against the power of majorities. "The Constitution is itself," as Hamilton put it in the *Federalist*, no. 84, "in every rational sense, and to every useful purpose, A BILL OF RIGHTS."

[52]See U.S. Constitution, Article I, sec. 9.

[53]Ibid.

[54]Alexander Hamilton, *Federalist*, no. 84. See the discussion in Herbert Storing, "The Constitution and the Bill of Rights," in Harmon, *Essays*, pp. 32–48.

When conservatives like Bork treat rights as islands surrounded by a sea of government powers, they precisely reverse the view of the Founders as enshrined in the Constitution, wherein government powers are limited and specified and rendered as islands surrounded by a sea of individual rights.

To help quiet the fears of the Anti-Federalists, the proponents of the Constitution did eventually propose a Bill of Rights in the first Congress. But the logic of limited government was not overturned. Madison imbedded this logic in the Bill of Rights itself. Thus, to the first eight amendments, which specify various liberties to be protected against government, were added the Ninth Amendment, which explicitly denies that popular rights could be limited to those enumerated in the Constitution, and the Tenth Amendment, which reserves all powers not delegated to the federal government to the states and the people.

Given that the Founders originally believed that the need for a Bill of Rights had been preempted by the limited nature of national government powers, constitutional interpreters should not be so preoccupied with the Bill of Rights as to neglect the power-limiting logic of the Constitution itself. Whereas the president is granted "The Executive Power," and the courts "The Judicial Power," Congress is conspicuously given only "all legislative powers *herein granted*" (emphasis added). Legislative powers are specifically enumerated and not general.

Just how narrowly the specific grants of legislative powers should be read is a hard question of constitutional interpretation, a harder question than the conservatives admit. Article I, section 8, of the Constitution enumerates Congress's powers. The first eight powers concern commerce broadly: the powers to tax, to borrow money on credit, to regulate commerce, to establish uniform rules for naturalization and bankruptcy, to "coin money," to punish counterfeiting, to establish post offices, and to grant exclusive patents and copyrights. The other powers granted to Congress provide for the establishment of lower courts, for the governing of the District of Columbia, and, most importantly, for national security. At the end of section 8 stands the "necessary and proper" clause: Congress may "make all laws which shall be necessary and proper for carrying into Execution the foregoing Powers, and all other Powers vested by this Constitution in the Government of the United States."

The "necessary and proper" clause certainly allows Congress to do many things incidentally required to carry out the enumerated powers. In the early years of the republic, however, a much broader way of reading the seemingly narrow grants of legislative power was devised by Chief Justice Marshall.

The case of *McCulloch* v. *Maryland* raised the question of the constitutionality of a bill establishing a national bank.[55] Nowhere does the Constitution specifically give this power to Congress, and Thomas Jefferson, among others, argued that the establishment of a bank was beyond the powers of the national government.

Marshall's decision in *McCulloch,* one of the most important ever handed down, was based on the claim that the specific grants of legislative power in Article I, section 8, are the "great outlines" of Congress's power. But the specific enumerations do not exhaust the means by which Congress may pursue its great ends. The very "nature" of a Constitution, said Marshall, requires that it avoid "the prolixity of a legal code," its "great outlines should be marked, its important objects designated, and the main ingredients which compose those objects deduced from the nature of the objects themselves." Although the Constitution does not specifically grant the power to establish a national bank, this power is, said Marshall, a legitimate means that facilitates the achievement of ends that are granted: to lay and collect taxes, to coin money, to regulate commerce, and to support armies and navies.

The logic of Marshall's argument is almost universally accepted today. At the time, however, it was rejected by such notables as

[55]4 Wheaton 316 (1819).

Madison and Jefferson. They argued that Marshall's logic permitted Congress "to take possession of a boundless field of power, no longer susceptible of any definition," making a mockery of the idea of limited government.[56] This is not quite true. Even on Marshall's expansive reading, the great ends of the national government remain limited; Congress may not use its powers as "pretexts" to pursue ends not related to the promotion of commerce and national security.[57]

Despite its nearly universal acceptance, Marshall's logic is not unassailable. It is not true, for instance, that the Constitution's language on Congress's powers speaks only in "great outlines" and does "not enumerate means." Consider the following clause in Article I, section 8: Congress may "promote the Progress of Science and useful Arts, by securing for limited Times to Authors and Inventors the exclusive Right to their respective Writings and Discoveries." This clause specifies both the end and the means, and it does so rather specifically. Even when read in light of the "necessary and proper" clause, it clearly implies that Congress may not promote "the Progress of Science and useful Arts" by means other than those specified. The part of the clause following the word "by" specifies how Congress may promote science and the arts, and it would be useless and inexplicable if Congress were free to choose any convenient means to that end. Thus, it is hard to see how one could establish the constitutionality of, say, the National Science Foundation.

Marshall's claim that the enumeration of powers in Article I, section 8, speaks only in "great outlines" or of vast powers is also untrue. Powers are listed that could have been derived by extrapolations less significant than that supporting the power to establish a national bank. After providing that an army and navy can be raised and supported, for instance, section 8 provides the

[56]Thomas Jefferson, as quoted in Gerald Gunther, *Cases and Materials on Constitutional Law* (Mineola, N.Y.: Foundation Press, 1980), p. 95.

[57]See Barber, chap. 4.

power "to make Rules for the government and regulation of the land and naval forces."

There is certainly much more to be said on both sides of this important issue. Short shrift has been given here to Marshall's complex argument, to the arguments in the *Federalist* that might support his position, and to the formidable scholarly works that have defended his position. The purpose of this discussion is certainly not to prove that *McCulloch* was wrongly decided. Rather, it is, first, to make clear that Marshall's reasoning about Congress's powers, upon which a vast edifice of constitutional law has been erected, does not depend on any cramped literalism or on a search for an original intention. (If judges stuck "close to the text and its clear implications" when interpreting powers, as Bork says they should when interpreting rights, the national government would be very severely constrained indeed.)

A second purpose here is to make clear that, contrary to the claim of such conservatives as Bork, the Constitution does not establish a basically majoritarian democracy of broad powers and few minority rights. On its face, the Constitution's language with regard to powers is restrictive, and even on Marshall's expansive reading, national powers remain limited. Marshall's reasoning in *McCulloch* stretches, but does not fundamentally overturn, the logic of enumerated powers and limited legislative ends. And what we need to do next is note the expansive language of those provisions protecting individual liberties in the Bill of Rights.

The Constitution lends explicit support to the values of economic freedom, private security, property rights, and liberty of contract. Article I, section 10, prohibits any state "Law impairing the Obligation of Contracts." The Third Amendment protects the sanctity of the home against the quartering of troops, and the Fourth Amendment protects "The right of the people to be secure in their persons, houses, papers, and effects, against unreasonable searches and seizures." Personal security and privacy are thus clearly linked with property ownership. The Fifth Amendment brings life, liberty, and property under the protection of "due process of law," and this guarantee is explicitly extended to the states by the Fourteenth Amendment. The Fifth Amendment also requires that private property may be taken only for public use and with "just compensation."

There is, of course, considerable textual support in the Constitution for other, noneconomic liberties, including religious freedom and freedom of speech, of the press, and of assembly. The founding document also protects the many privileges and immunities associated with the rule of law and with fair proceedings in criminal cases, in the Fifth, Sixth, Seventh, and Eighth amendments. The Ninth Amendment, as noted, explicitly warns against construing the "enumeration" of "certain rights" to "deny or disparage others retained by the people." And the Tenth Amendment emphasizes that the powers of the federal government are limited to those "delegated" to it (though, of course, not necessarily to those expressly or explicitly enumerated). The Bill of Rights closes with the reminder that powers not delegated are "reserved to the States respectively, or to the people."

The Constitution is basically concerned not simply with empowering the people's representatives to govern, but with checking and limiting the powers of legislative majorities in a host of important ways, both procedurally and substantively (or on both the "input" and the "output" sides). The New Right's preoccupation with the legitimacy of judicial review ignores the fact that in a system of limited government, the exercise of legislative power itself demands positive constitutional support. Legislators and executives are bound, no less than judges are, to carry out their constitutional mandate. All who take an oath to support the Constitution as supreme law have an obligation to conscientiously strive toward its ends and purposes and not just to avoid breaking its most obvious commands. There is no presumption in the Constitution in favor of legislatures and against judges, or in favor of majority power and against individual rights and liberties. Judicial review is not an anomalous blotch on a democratic scheme of government. Contrary to what the conservatives hold, judicial review is an integral part of a scheme of constitutionally limited government.

How best to reconcile the logic of *McCulloch* with the Constitution's commitment to a broad expanse of individual rights is a hard question to be confronted by judges in adjudicating cases, and also by legislators and others when serving as conscientious interpreters. If one accepts the power-expanding logic of *McCulloch* and yet also construes rights expansively (as commanded by the Ninth Amendment), one has to undertake the hard, but far from impossible, task of drawing lines between the powers of the national government and the rights of individuals, and between the powers of the national government and the reserved powers of the states. What must be utterly unacceptable, to any conscientious interpreter, is a jurisprudence that ignores broad individual rights so well anchored in the Constitution.

IV. Morality and Constitutional Law

Before considering what, in substance, a principled constitutional jurisprudence should be, it is necessary to contend with the New Right's skeptical, derisive attitude toward the judicial invocation of moral principles. The New Right's moral skepticism is utterly implausible, ignoble, and deeply at odds with America's morally robust constitutional tradition.

Bork insists, uncontroversially, that judicial decisions must rest on "reasoned opinions," that is, a "legitimate" court must have "a valid theory, derived from the Constitution" to justify its actions.[58] Bork's view of what constitutes a constitutional principle is, however, extremely narrow: valid constitutional principles are drawn only from the text interpreted in light of specific historical intentions; the "framers' intentions with respect to freedoms are the sole legitimate premise from which constitutional analysis may proceed."[59] On Bork's reading, therefore, the equal protection clause of the Fourteenth Amendment has two requirements: "formal procedural equality," as the bare text clearly requires, and no government discrimination along racial lines, because a concern with race is revealed by the history of the Fourteenth Amendment.

Cut loose from plain text and historical intentions, there is, for Bork, "no principled way of saying which . . . inequalities are permissible."[60] Beyond text and historical intention are "matters of morality," which "belong . . . to the political community."[61] Political morality is of no help in deciding constitutional questions

[58]Bork, "Neutral Principles," p. 3.
[59]Bork, *Tradition*, p. 10.
[60]Bork, "Neutral Principles," p. 11.
[61]Ibid., p. 12.

because, says Bork, any system of "moral and ethical values . . . has no objective or intrinsic validity of its own"; there is, in effect, no right and wrong because all that can be said about morality is that "men can and do differ."[62] As if to make moral skepticism or subjectivism official U.S. government policy, Attorney General Meese approvingly quotes Bork's aphorism: "The judge who looks outside the Constitution always looks inside himself and nowhere else."[63]

Bork's skepticism turns to cynicism when he reduces all moral claims to claims for "gratification": "Every clash between a minority claiming freedom and a majority claiming power to regulate involves a choice between the gratifications of two groups."[64] When examining Griswold v. Connecticut, a case in which married couples asserted, as a matter of constitutional and political morality, the right to use contraceptives in the privacy of their own home, Bork sees no serious moral problem but only a question of "sexual gratification." Since there is no principled way, according to Bork, to discriminate between kinds of "gratification," the majority should have its way.[65] Bork would extend First Amendment protections only to political speech that is within the bounds of the established legal order; he would extend no judicial protection to academic, literary, or any other forms of expression.[66]

Chief Justice Rehnquist, generally considered an intellectual leader of the conservative bloc on the Supreme Court, shares Bork's moral skepticism: "Many of us necessarily feel strongly and deeply about our own moral judgments, but they remain only personal moral judgments until in some way given the sanction of law."[67] What Rehnquist, like Bork, gives us is moral skep-

[62]Ibid., p. 10.
[63]Meese, Federalist Society address, p. 11.
[64]Bork, "Neutral Principles," p. 9.
[65]Ibid., p. 11; and see Griswold v. Connecticut, 381 U.S. 479 (1965).
[66]Bork, "Neutral Principles," p. 20.
[67]William H. Rehnquist, "The Notion of a Living Constitution," Texas Law Review 54 (1976): 704.

ticism in the service of majoritarianism, masquerading as an innocent respect for the constitutional text.

Judge Posner expresses a similar skepticism about "value
judgments":

> [It is] inevitable that many judicial decisions will be based on
> value judgments rather than technical determinations; and
> decisions so made are by definition not scientific, and there-
> fore are not readily falsifiable and hence not readily verifiable
> either—and as a consequence are not always profitably
> discussable.[68]

Although Posner's skepticism has a scientific gloss, and his position is arguably more sophisticated than Bork's, he agrees with
Bork in urging judges to confine themselves to principles that
have "public approbation" and "values that are widely . . . held"
in the community.[69]

The New Right's attitude to rights claims appears to have the
advantage of a tough-minded, down-to-earth, realism. Bork makes
much of preferring the "common sense of the people" to the
"theorists of moral abstraction," to "intellectuals," and to "what-
have-you philosophy."[70] But the appearance of realism is spurious, for Americans could not make sense of their traditions,
practices, and habitual ways of thinking, acting, and judging, or
of the Constitution, if they accepted the New Right's radical moral
skepticism. Indeed, it is hard to see how one could reconcile the
New Right's apparently principled preference for democracy with
its moral skepticism. (After all, why should anyone, except on
the basis of a principle of moral equality, prefer the gratifications
of the majority to a minority? Why should we prefer democracy
to totalitarianism?)

The apparent lesson of the New Right's derision of rights and

[68]Richard A. Posner, "The Meaning of Judicial Self-Restraint," *Indiana Law Journal*
59 (1983): 6.

[69]Ibid., pp. 10, 23.

[70]Bork, *Tradition*, pp. 7–11.

moral reflection is that moral claims can be ignored because they are no more than the way that "intellectuals" dress up their preferences and gratifications. In reducing rights claims to demands for "gratification," the New Right theorists destroy the distinction between moral reasons and mere arbitrary preferences. And as Sotirios Barber points out, to insist that a community's enforced ethical values need express no more than the merely subjective preferences of the majority is to put forward "a sophisticated version of the maxim that might makes right."[71]

In telling the majority, those with the strength of numbers, that morality may be ignored (because moral reasons are mere preferences), the New Right calls upon what is worst, not what is best, in the public. The Framers recognized this stance; indeed, they feared it. They feared the untutored, unrefined "prejudices" of the people, and they regarded those who would flatter and enflame these prejudices as demagogues.

The Framers feared the "passions" of the people, and they argued that "the reason, alone, of the public . . . ought to control and regulate the government."[72] The Framers were not simple democrats, but republicans who rejected the idea that popular government was necessarily good government. They sought to ensure that political power would be in the hands of the wisest members of the community and not those most responsive to popular prejudices: "The republican principle demands that the deliberate sense of the community should govern."[73] And, unlike Bork and others in today's New Right, the Framers were neither morally skeptical nor derisive of abstract ideas. For what else but abstract ideas are the "self-evident" truths of the Declaration of Independence? What else but philosophical principles are "una-

---

[71]Sotirios Barber, "Judge Bork's Constitution," in *Courts, Judges, and Politics*, 3d ed., ed. Walter F. Murphy and C. Herman Pritchett (New York: Random House, forthcoming), pp. 691–95. Barber also has pointed out to the present author that Bork's position is essentially the same as that of Thrasymachus, in Plato's *Republic*, who argued against Socrates that justice is no more than the interest of the stronger.

[72]*Federalist*, no. 49.

[73]*Federalist*, no. 71.

lienable Rights" that belong naturally to all men? And how else, except as the assertion of an abstract moral claim, can one understand the Framers' assertion that "Justice is the end of government"?[74]

Fortunately, despite its apparent tough-mindedness, the New Right's conception of morality is so counterintuitive that hardly anyone would accept it and so implausible that no one should. Who really believes that moral claims express only desires for "gratification," as Bork asserts? To accept Bork's position, one would have to believe that there is no moral difference between the "gratification" of a murderer and the "gratification" of his potential victim who wishes to live. According to Bork, "Anything some people want has, to that degree, social value."[75] But what of the desires of the rapist, the thief, and the arsonist? Do these desires have social value? And do they fail to win moral approval and become lawful only because they are the desires of minorities?

Contrary to Bork, the truth is that we can and do distinguish between mere gratifications and genuine moral claims all the time. We say with moral confidence that the gratifications of those who enjoy murdering, raping, stealing, burning other people's homes, or violating rights in other ways count for nothing. We believe in fundamental rights, to freedom of conscience and of speech, to life and to at least some forms of privacy, on the basis of moral reason and not on the basis of absurd calculations about net gratifications.

The New Right's moral theory is nothing if not audacious, but it would take more than audacity to seriously argue either that the Framers of the Constitution shared this deep skepticism or that the American people do so today. The Framers were suspicious of democracy and confident that certain standards of political morality transcend the will of any majority. And they sought,

[74]*Federalist*, no. 51.
[75]Bork, "Neutral Principles," p. 29.

in the deliberations on the ratification of the Constitution, to direct the public's attention toward reflection on justice and away from arbitrary preferences and immediate "gratifications": the conduct of this country would decide, said Hamilton in the first paragraph of the first *Federalist*, "whether societies of men are capable or not of establishing good government from reflection and choice" rather than "accident and force." And Thomas Paine expressed the faith of his generation when he claimed, "The Independence of America was accompanied by a Revolution in the principles and practices of Governments. . . . Government founded on a moral theory . . . on the indefeasible hereditary Rights of Man, is now revolving from West to East."[76]

Bork basks in his derision of moral abstractions and claims that his posture expresses reverence for the founders and our political tradition. But moral abstractions, such as rights and justice, did play a central role in the minds of the Founders and do form an essential part of America's constitutional tradition.

The main sources of the political ideas of the founding generation were the legal authorities Edward Coke and William Blackstone and the great classical liberal political theorist John Locke.[77] All three accepted the political centrality of "natural law" morality. Coke and Locke, in particular, continually stressed that moral standards defining individual rights were binding on all political actors, including popular majorities and legislatures.

Most importantly for the argument at hand, in the period of the revolution, the "higher law," or natural moral law, was held to embody judicially enforceable limits on legislatures and posi-

[76]Thomas Paine, *The Rights of Man*, quoted in Thomas Pangle, "Patriotism American Style," *National Review*, November 29, 1985, pp. 30–34.

[77]On the influence of Locke, see Bernard Bailyn, *The Ideological Origins of the American Revolution* (Cambridge: Harvard University Press, 1982), especially pp. 27–28. On Locke and Coke, see Edward S. Corwin, *The "Higher Law" Background of American Constitutionalism* (Ithaca, N.Y.: Cornell University Press, 1979). On Blackstone's teaching on "natural law" and his influence on the Founders, see W. A. Mell, "James Wilson, Alexander Hamilton, and William Blackstone," doctoral dissertation, University of Oregon, 1976 (reprinted by University Microfilms, Ann Arbor, Mich., 1980).

tive law. Coke, whose *Commentaries* Jefferson called "the universal lawbook of students," argued that "when an act of Parliament is against common right and reason, or repugnant, or impossible to be performed, the common law will control it and adjudge such act to be void."[78]

John Locke, the political thinker who exercised the greatest influence on the republic's founding generation, argued that men gave up none of their natural rights when entering political society; they gave to government only the power to better "preserve" their natural rights to "liberty and property."[79] Thomas Jefferson echoed Lockean theory when, in 1816, he asserted,

> Our legislators are not sufficiently apprised of the rightful limits of their power; that their true office is to declare and enforce only our natural rights and duties, and to take none of them from us. . . . When the laws have declared and enforced all this, they have fulfilled their functions; and the idea is quite unfounded that on entering society we give up any natural right.[80]

Not all the Founders adhered strictly, even in theory, to Lockeanism, and none of them acted solely on the basis of morality. Prudence, together with forms of political wisdom beyond moral reflection, comes into play in any successful act of statecraft. These facts notwithstanding, it is safe to say that the Founders did not doubt the existence of moral rights that bind popular governments. The Constitution itself, moreover, does not confer rights, but only "secures" them. And the Ninth Amendment explicitly calls upon constitutional interpreters not to "deny or disparage" the existence of rights not stated explicitly in the Constitution. By implication, then, the Constitution calls upon all citizens and public officials to reflect upon the rights that

[78]Corwin, p. 42.

[79]John Locke, *Two Treatises on Government*, Second Treatise, ed. Peter Laslett (New York: New American Library, 1965), par. 131, pp. 398–99.

[80]Thomas Jefferson, as quoted in Murphy, "Art," p. 140.

people have even in the absence of explicit political acknowledgment. The Ninth Amendment calls upon conscientious interpreters to reflect upon natural rights and so to engage in moral theory.

The New Right's moral skepticism, as well as its disparaging attitude toward rights not explicitly stated in the text of the Constitution, find little support in the ideas of the Founders or in the text of the Constitution. Not surprisingly, then, judicially enforceable moral principles, even those not explicitly stated in the Constitution, have played an important role throughout U.S. history. Early on, Justice Chase invoked, in *Calder* v. *Bull,* "the general principles of law and reason" that constrain legislators even in the absence of explicit constitutional provisions.[81]

Chief Justice Marshall, an ardent nationalist, could have struck down Georgia's revocation of a land grant in *Fletcher* v. *Peck* by invoking only the Constitution's contracts clause. Instead, he went beyond the text of the Constitution and engaged in a considerable discussion of "the great principles of justice, whose authority is universally acknowledged."[82] Seventeen years later, in *Ogden* v. *Saunders*, Marshall invoked the "abstract philosophy" of natural rights: "Individuals do not derive from government their right to contract, but bring that right with them into society. . . . [E]very man retains [the right] to acquire property, to dispose of that property according to his own judgment, and to pledge himself for a future act."[83]

When one thinks of the American political tradition at its best, Abraham Lincoln must rank alongside the greatest of the Founders. Lincoln's political morality, his central concern with human equality as a moral principle, stands sharply at odds with Bork's skepticism. In the Gettysburg Address, Lincoln described the central proposition of the Declaration of Independence, to which

[81] 3 Dall. 395 (1798).
[82] 3 L.Ed. 162 (1810).
[83] 2 Wheaton 213 (1827).

the nation was dedicated at its birth, as "an abstract truth applicable to all men and all times." Lincoln, unlike Bork, held that right and wrong depend on standards of judgment independent of mere opinion. What Lincoln would have thought of the assertion that the gratifications of slave traders and slaves, for instance, are not morally distinguishable, or are distinguishable only quantitatively, may easily be inferred from his Peoria speech of 1854:

All these free blacks are the descendants of slaves, or have been slaves themselves, and they would be now, but for *something* which has operated on their white owners, inducing them, at vast pecuniary sacrifices, to liberate them. What is that *something?* Is there any mistaking it? In all these cases it is your sense of justice, and human sympathy, continually telling you, that the poor negro has some natural right to himself—that those who deny it, and make merchandise of him, deserve kicking, contempt, and death.[84]

After the Civil War, the development of the doctrine of "substantive due process" carried forward the "higher law" tradition in the form of judicially protected economic liberties. Accordingly, Bork's disparaging attitude toward moral rights neglects not only the ideas of the Framers but also important aspects of the American constitutional and political tradition.

Bork is on firmer ground when he charges that in recent times the Supreme Court, in defining values sufficiently "fundamental" to warrant judicial protection, has neglected some rights, especially economic ones, for no good reason. In this way, the Court has indeed been "political"; it has ignored the high standing of economic rights in the Constitution's text, in our political tradition, and in moral theory. The modern Court has erected a

[84]Abraham Lincoln, speech delivered at Peoria, Ill., 1854, as quoted in Harry V. Jaffa, *Crisis of the House Divided* (Seattle: University of Washington Press, 1973), p. 312. For a discussion of Lincoln's view of the moral status of the Declaration of Independence, see Jaffa, chap. 14; and Gary J. Jacobsohn, "Abraham Lincoln 'On this Question of Judicial Authority': The Theory of Constitutional Aspiration," *Western Political Quarterly* 36, no. 1 (1983): 52–70.

constitutional double standard by giving high place to "personal rights" while neglecting economic rights that are at least as well founded in the Constitution.

The Supreme Court can and should be criticized for the narrow way in which it has defined those "fundamental" values and "preferred" freedoms worthy of judicial protection. It should not be concluded, however, that the active judicial defense of liberty and rights should be abandoned, for this defense is supported by the Constitution's text, by the ideas of the Framers, and by our political tradition. The proper course, it seems, is for conscientious interpreters of the Constitution to correct, not abandon, judicial activism.

There is clearly a close fit between the three levels of the New Right's jurisprudence. The resort to historical intentions to construe rights narrowly is supported by the preference for majority power over individual liberty, and that in turn is supported by moral skepticism. And yet at each level, the New Right's position is diametrically opposed to the ideas of the Framers, to the text of the Constitution, and to morality itself, which limits and defines our ultimate political duties. Having proceeded thus far in the task of clearing the ground, it is now worthwhile to consider briefly the possible form of a principled judicial activism.

V. Principled Judicial Activism

Assuming the preceding critique of the jurisprudence of the New Right is sound, there is a need for a constitutional vision with a robust conception of judicially enforceable rights grounded in the text of the Constitution, in sound moral thinking, and in our political tradition. A principled judicial activism would overcome the incoherence of the modern Court's double standard.

A principled jurisprudence would draw upon all the sources available and relevant to the task of constitutional interpretation. First and foremost among these sources are the text and structure of the Constitution and the nature of the institutions established by the document. However, both the text, especially the preamble (which Lino Graglia dismisses as a mere "rhetorical flourish"[85]) and the Ninth Amendment, and our tradition direct us beyond the rights explicitly stated in the document, so it is not possible to dispense with an understanding of the morality of individual rights. For the conscientious interpreter, moral theory is an aid to, not a substitute for, interpretation of the text. Given the openness of the text to a morality of broad individual rights, the two are complementary rather than competing, and our moral duties and our duties as citizens overlap. (Robert Bork once advocated roughly the kind of principled activism being advanced here; he allowed that a "legitimate judicial activism" would give "content to the concept of natural rights in a case-by-case interpretation of the Constitution."[86])

The jurisprudence of the modern Supreme Court has developed in response to the perceived illegitimacy of the Court's

[85]Graglia, "Would the Court," p. 815.
[86]See Robert H. Bork, "The Supreme Court Needs a New Philosophy," *Fortune* 78 (December 1968): 138 ff.

efforts, over many years, to develop principled ways of limiting the regulatory powers of the federal and state governments in the economic sphere. The Court's efforts in the economic sphere were directed at imposing limits on Congress's regulatory powers under the commerce clause and at defining individual economic liberties enforceable against the states under the Fourteenth Amendment's due process clause. Despite the fact that most constitutional scholars on both the left and the right now argue that the Court should give Congress and the states a free hand in the economic sphere, the Court's efforts, while far from perfect, were on the whole legitimate and principled exercises in constitutional interpretation. (Richard Epstein, Bernard Siegan, and Martin Schapiro are exceptions to the overwhelming, but I believe ill-founded, consensus on this point.[87])

In the late 19th and early 20th centuries, the Court forged distinctions to define and limit Congress's power to "regulate Commerce . . . among the several States."[88] Of particular importance was the distinction made between commerce and production that placed regulation of production beyond Congress's power and among the reserved powers of the states.[89] These distinctions were swept away when the Court moved to accept the constitutionality of the New Deal.[90] However, any conscientious interpreter of the Constitution must feel uncomfortable with a commerce power so extensive that it sacrifices other values with high

[87]For a lengthy analysis of the relevant case law, see Bernard Siegan, *Economic Liberties and the Constitution* (Chicago: University of Chicago, 1980). See also Martin Schapiro, "The Constitution and Economic Liberties," in Harmon, *Essays*, pp. 74–98. An important addition to this literature is Richard Epstein, *Takings: Private Property and the Power of Eminent Domain* (Cambridge: Harvard University Press, 1985).

[88]U.S. Constitution, Article I, section 8.

[89]*U.S. v. E. C. Knight*, 156 U.S. 1 (1895).

[90]See *N.L.R.B. v. Jones & Laughlin Steel Co.*, 301 U.S. 1 (1937); and *U.S. v. Darby*, 312 U.S. 100 (1941).

constitutional standing, or with a commerce power used pretextually to pursue ends unrelated to commerce.[91]

Consider the case of an Ohio farmer named Filburn who sowed 23 acres of wheat wholly for consumption on his farm. He was fined by Franklin Roosevelt's Department of Agriculture, however, for harvesting in excess of his quota, which the department had set at 11.1 acres.[92] The New Deal's Agricultural Adjustment Act of 1938 gave the secretary of agriculture the power to establish such quotas to help regulate supply and stabilize prices. Although there was no "commerce" involved in Filburn's activity, the Court ruled in *Wickard* v. *Filburn* that his activities "affected commerce" and that excess supply constituted an "obstruction to commerce."[93]

The problem with *Wickard*, of course, is that it sacrifices property rights closely bound up with personal autonomy to a policy rather loosely related to Congress's commerce power. Long before, Justice Holmes had warned, in *Northern Securities Co.* v. *U.S.*, that the logic of indirect effects on a "national market" had no limit: "Almost anything—marriage, birth, death, may in some manner affect commerce."[94] However, without the sorts of defining and limiting distinctions that the Court has since abandoned, it is hard to see why marriage and divorce should not fall under commercial regulation as well.

Besides the limits placed on the commerce power, the old Court also deployed against the states the doctrine of "substantive due process," a doctrine now identified most closely with the case of *Lochner* v. *New York*.[95] In *Lochner*, the Court struck down a New York statute limiting the working hours of bakery employees as

---

[91]For a pretextual use of the commerce power to suppress lotteries and thereby pursue an end subsumed by the states' reserved police powers, see *Champion* v. *Ames*, 188 U.S. 321 (1903). For the apparent abandonment of Marshall's pretextual limitation, forged in *McCulloch*, see *U.S.* v. *Darby*, 312 U.S. 100 (1941).

[92]*Wickard* v. *Filburn*, 317 U.S. 111 (1942).

[93]Ibid.

[94]193 U.S. 197 (1904).

[95]198 U.S. 45 (1905).

an abridgment of "liberty of contract." The modern Court has not abandoned the idea that the Fourteenth Amendment, which says, "No State shall . . . deprive any person of life, liberty, or property without due process of law," implies that there are substantive limits on the ways in which the state can interfere with private relations. The Court has simply shifted its inquiries away from the economic sphere. When it comes to state economic regulation, the Court requires nothing more than the merest "rationality" to justify restrictions on individual liberty. In instances when legislators have not put forward a rational basis for restrictions on economic liberty, the Court has simply hypothesized its own rationale, as in *Williamson* v. *Lee Optical* and *Ferguson* v. *Skrupka*.[96]

The modern Court has largely abandoned the protection of substantive economic values, but it has not abandoned fundamental values altogether. The Court closely scrutinizes legislation touching on a list of "preferred freedoms," such as the right to freedom of speech, of religion, and of the press, and more recently the right to privacy and the equal protection of the laws.

The Constitution, as already noted, manifests a basic concern with protecting a wide range of human freedoms. Government powers are limited, and the Ninth Amendment explicitly states that people have rights not explicitly mentioned in the document. Judges cannot flinch, therefore, at the task of applying the same expansive logic to individual rights that *McCulloch* applies to government powers. An excellent case in point is *Griswold* v. *Connecticut*, which Bork derides as an arbitrary judicial creation of a new right.[97] *Griswold* struck down a Connecticut statute that made it illegal for married couples to use contraceptives. The Court based its decision on an implicit constitutional right to zones of privacy, which emanate from, or form "penumbras" around, the specific guarantees of the Bill of Rights. As Justice

[96]348 U.S. 343 (1955) and 372 U.S. 726 (1963), respectively.
[97]381 U.S. 479 (1965).

Douglas argued, these implicit, penumbral rights, including one protecting the privacy of the marriage relationship, help give life and substance to express guarantees:

Various guarantees create zones of privacy. The right of association contained in the penumbra of the First Amendment is one, as we have seen. The Third Amendment in its protection against the quartering of soldiers "in any house" in time of peace without the consent of the owner is another facet of that privacy. The Fourth Amendment explicitly affirms the "right of the people to be secure in their persons, houses, papers, and effects against unreasonable searches and seizures." The Fifth Amendment in its Self-Incrimination Clause enables the citizen to create a zone of privacy which government may not force him to surrender to his detriment.

Justice Goldberg, concurring, emphasized the importance of taking the Ninth Amendment seriously: "The Ninth Amendment shows a belief of the Constitution's authors that fundamental rights exist that are not expressly enumerated in the first eight amendments. . . . [T]he subsequently enacted 14th Amendment prohibits the states as well from abridging fundamental personal liberties."

Most commentators on the left applaud the Court's shift from protecting economic values to protecting noneconomic ones such as privacy. Conservatives like Bork, on the other hand, see the new jurisprudence as no better than the old. Conservatives want the Court to abandon the protection of not only economic liberties but of all "fundamental" interests or "substantive" values other than those explicitly stated in the constitutional text and originally intended by the Framers.

In a sense, the conservatives do have a point, for both the new "activist" jurisprudence and the old are flawed. In both cases, the choice of values to be protected is partial, unprincipled, and, therefore, political. The "Old Men," as the justices supporting the majority position in the *Lochner*-era Court were known, failed

53

to adequately recognize the high place that the Constitution gives to such noneconomic liberties as freedom of speech.[98] The modern Court errs, likewise, in arbitrarily neglecting values that have a high place in the Constitution's scheme of values. Nevertheless, these errors can be corrected without abandoning the active judicial protection of individual rights. The error in both cases is not that constitutionally protected liberties are judicially enforced, but that not all constitutionally protected liberties are enforced. Worse than the application of the double standard would be to suppose, as does Bork, that American citizens have no judicially enforceable rights except those explicitly stated in the Constitution and specifically intended by the Framers.

The modern Court's double standard, which neglects economic liberties and protects other "personal" liberties, like privacy, is incoherent and untenable. It flies in the face of the plain words of the Constitution, ignores important aspects of our legal and political traditions, and fails to recognize that economic and other "favored" liberties are mutually interdependent and commonly grounded on an even more basic, implicit constitutional principle: the dignity of persons who are bearers of broad rights and capable of responsible self-government.

The underlying logic of *Griswold* is essentially correct, though Douglas's execution leaves much to be desired. Just as *McCulloch* sought to interpret and enforce the principles and purposes underlying the Constitution's enumeration of Congress's powers, so *Griswold* seeks to enforce the principles and purposes underlying the Constitution's specific guarantees of rights. Conscientious interpreters cannot shirk either the project of *McCulloch* or the project of *Griswold*. From specific textual provisions, structures, and underlying purposes, conscientious interpreters must strive toward a complete and defensible theory of the Constitution as the best means to achieve our best understanding of its

---

[98]See, among other cases, *Schenck* v. *U.S.*, 249 U.S. 47 (1919); *Abrams* v. *U.S.*, 250 U.S. 616 (1919); and *Whitney* v. *California*, 274 U.S. 357 (1927).

great ends: "to form a more perfect Union, establish Justice, insure domestic Tranquility, provide for the common defence, promote the general Welfare, and secure the Blessings of Liberty to ourselves and our Posterity." Only by fusing constitutional and moral theory can interpreters at once vindicate and justify the Constitution's authority as supreme law; only in this way do interpreters help insure that our republic will remain worthy of allegiance and that we will be governed by more than power and mere willfullness.

Constitutional commentators on and off the bench are coming to recognize that the new double standard is no better than the old. They perceive that what is needed is a jurisprudence that acknowledges the constitutional status of both economic and other important liberties. As Justice Stewart pointed out in *Lynch v. Household Finance Corporation:*

> The dichotomy between personal liberties and property rights is a false one. Property does not have rights. People have rights. The right to enjoy property without unlawful deprivation, no less than the right to speak out or the right to travel, is, in truth, a "personal" right. . . . [A] fundamental interdependence exists between the personal right to liberty and the personal right in property. Neither could have meaning without the other. That rights in property are basic civil rights has long been recognized.[99]

Although the Court of the *Lochner* era may justly be accused of inadequate concern with noneconomic freedoms, it did take the important step of holding that the word "liberty" in the Fourteenth Amendment's due process clause includes the liberty of speech.[100] Even the crustiest of the "Old Men," Justice McReynolds, recognized the close relation between economic and other personal liberties and thus pointed the way toward a principled

[99]405 U.S. 538, 552 (1972). Stewart cites Locke, John Adams, and Blackstone on this point.
[100]*Gitlow* v. *New York,* 268 U.S. 652 (1925).

synthesis. In *Meyer* v. *Nebraska*, the Court overturned the conviction of a German-language teacher under a statute prohibiting the teaching of foreign languages to young children.[101] Justice McReynolds articulated a broad conception of the liberty protected by the Fourteenth Amendment:

Without doubt, it denotes not merely freedom from bodily restraint, but also the right of the individual to contract, to engage in any of the common occupations of life, to acquire useful knowledge, to marry, establish a home and bring up children, to worship God according to the dictates of his conscience, and generally to enjoy those privileges long recognized at common law as essential to the orderly pursuit of happiness by free men.[102]

McReynolds correctly linked the autonomy and intellectual freedom of parents and students with the "economic" right of language teachers to pursue their calling.[103]

More recently, in *Moore* v. *East Cleveland*, a city zoning ordinance limiting occupancy of dwellings to a single, "nuclear" family was successfully challenged by a grandmother living with her two grandchildren.[104] In his plurality opinion, Justice Powell argued from the traditional importance of autonomous family life, and he denied the state's authority to require "all to live in certain narrowly defined family patterns." Justice Stevens's concurring opinion explicitly linked the values at stake with the grandmother's property rights, in particular her common-law right to decide who resides on her property. He found no substantial relation between the ordinance and the state's police powers to regulate health, safety, and morals. By placing the act beyond the state's legitimate powers, Stevens found it a "taking" of property without just compensation or due process.

[101]262 U.S. 390 (1923).
[102]262 U.S. 399 (1923).
[103]See also *Pierce* v. *Society of Sisters*, 268 U.S. 510 (1925).
[104]431 U.S. 494 (1977).

56

Bork, as noted later in this discussion, charges that a political regime that elevates respect for individual rights to a constitutional command sacrifices the community's public morality to moral relativism. In fact, respecting the whole range of human rights, including property rights, is the best way for a pluralistic society such as ours to express a public morality.

A recent Michigan case highlights the deep interdependence of property rights and the secure enjoyment of liberties associated with self-determination, or autonomy, and community. *Poletown Neighborhood Council* v. *City of Detroit* arose over the taking by eminent domain of an entire Detroit neighborhood that the General Motors Corporation wanted to raze for the construction of an automobile plant.[105] The Michigan Supreme Court refused to step in and protect the property owners in this ethnic working-class neighborhood despite state and federal constitutional requirements that land be taken only for "public use." Construing government powers broadly and individual rights narrowly, as Bork recommends, the Michigan Supreme Court said the Constitution would be satisfied because the seizure and transfer to General Motors would provide a "public benefit." However, if property rights are to count for so little in the face of a government pursuing policy ends, then families, communities, and the other traditional groups of which the New Right is so solicitous are all rendered insecure and vulnerable to political vagaries and the passions of the moment.

The New Right rejoinder to the argument for combining protections for a broad sphere of individual liberties, both economic and otherwise, would undoubtedly be that one should not combine both sorts of protections but reject both. The conservative strategy does avoid a constitutional and moral double standard, but at the expense of a total blindness to the constitutional status of a broad expanse of individual liberty.

[105]410 Mich. 616, 304 N.W. 2d 455 (1981).

VI. The Agenda of Principled Activism

"Principled activism" is a response to threats to the constitutional order from both the New Right and the left. Principled activism, as I have argued, seeks active judicial protection of civil and personal rights of the sort favored in recent decades by selective activists (such as Justice Brennan). It is equally committed, however, to the Constitution's obvious concern for economic liberty and property rights. So it rejects the New Right's wholesale moral skepticism as well as the left's untenable double standard of selective activism.

According to much current constitutional thought, laws restricting economic liberty or other liberties that fall outside a list of "preferred" or "fundamental" freedoms need only be "rational" to pass constitutional muster. But this minimal standard of judicial review has, as applied, become a mere pretense of review, a veritable blank check for state legislatures to deprive people of economic and other liberties with a "due process of law" that is mere form without substance. Under the guise of reviewing the rationality of government restrictions on disfavored liberties, the Court generally refuses critically to consider the government's arguments and evidence. To announce, as the Supreme Court has, that restrictions on economic and other liberties will be deemed acceptable without a meaningful inquiry into the quality of the case advanced to support these restrictions is to provide a cloak for unjust and arbitrary power.[106] Such power, as constitutionalists have long recognized, epitomizes government tyranny.

[106]The Court's refusal is manifested in an extreme deference to state infringements on liberty, requiring only the "rational basis test" to justify restrictions on economic and other liberties. See chap. 5 above, especially p. 52.

Once we acknowledge the Constitution's concern for a broad and inclusive range of liberties, the positive program of principled activism becomes apparent. Conscientious interpreters of the Constitution must reject the Court's effective refusal to review infringements on economic liberty and other liberties that fall reasonably within the Constitution's scheme of values. The consequence of a principled activism would be twofold. On the procedural side, judges would critically examine the reasons and the evidence offered to support restrictions on liberty; they would infuse a measure of real "critical bite" into their review of *all* government restrictions on constitutional liberty.[107] On the substantive side, principled activism would give greater weight to the interest in economic liberty and thus offer greater judicial protection to the whole range of individual liberties—economic, civil, and personal. Principled activism would require, at the very least, that governments provide "real and substantial" justification for restrictions on the full array of liberties protected by the Constitution's scheme of values.[108] Principled activism would help protect liberty and ensure reasonableness in all spheres of government.

We should be deeply disturbed by the failure of judges on the right and the left carefully to examine the reasons supporting restrictions on individual liberty, whether economic or personal. We pride ourselves, after all, on living under a constitutional regime, a government "of laws and not of men." If constitutionalism and the rule of law stand for anything, they stand for the idea that one system of law applies to government officials and citizens alike, and that citizens have a right to challenge governmental acts in an independent court of law.[109] To act in a manner

---

[107]See Gerald Gunther, *Constitutional Law*, 11th ed. (Mineola, N.Y.: Foundation Press, 1985), pp. 472–75. I have benefited from Gunther's discussion of ways to infuse "critical bite" into the minimal rationality standard of judicial review.

[108]In theory, the still-operative standard is *Nebbia* v. *New York*, 291 U.S. 502 (1934).

[109]See A. V. Dicey, *The Law of the Constitution* (Indianapolis: Liberty Classics, 1982), esp. chaps. 5 and 12.

worthy of constitutionalism and the rule of law, public officials must be prepared not merely to assert their power over others, but to justify their acts in constitutional terms to dissenting citizens.

The Constitution provides grounds for challenging acts of government. It specifies the powers of the federal government and recognizes that citizens have rights that no government may infringe upon. Judicial review by the courts provides a forum for reasoned argument between citizens and public officials about the best interpretation of constitutional rights and powers. Judicial review expresses our commitment to treat even the weak and powerless in a reasonable and justifiable manner. As such, it embodies the nation's determination to be governed by more than mere force. The power of the courts in this system of government stands for the special form of respect we pay to those on the losing side of legislative battles or those who feel victimized by public officials carrying out the law.

Independent courts of law exercising judicial review embody and sustain a commitment to reasonable self-government. To absolve public officials from having to articulate adequate reasons justifying application of coercive power is to tear at the heart of constitutionalism and the rule of law. What the nonactivists of the right and the selective activists of the left threaten is, ultimately, the core aspiration of our constitutional order: the promise of reasonable self-government. Not only liberty itself, then, but constitutionalism's core commitment to genuine reasonableness is threatened by the ersatz rationality standard.

This chapter examines two recent cases raising issues that bear on the status of economic liberty under the Constitution. In these cases narrow Court majorities (to the consternation of both the right and left wings of the Court) seemed to accept a "beefed up" standard of minimum rationality, a standard with the critical bite that principled activism demands. We also examine a case involving personal liberty in which the Court refused to recognize the right to privacy of homosexuals, and in so doing relied on a rationality test with no critical bite whatsoever. The issue raised in all these cases is the legitimacy and vitality of a minimal rationality standard of review with no critical bite—the mere "reasonableness" test that prevails in most decisions involving what the Court arbitrarily calls nonfundamental rights. Beefing up this standard is, I shall argue, the first important step on the road to a more principled judicial activism: one that is reasonable and that recognizes the proper weight of economic liberty and the full range of human interests protected by such personal rights as privacy.

The Court has often held that Congress's power to regulate commerce implies that states may not enact discriminatory measures or erect trade barriers favoring local economic interests or protecting local markets.[110] The Court's active deployment of the commerce clause as a means of restricting state economic regulation has been guided by the judgment that an underlying purpose of the commerce clause is to establish an integrated national economy. This in turn reflects an original judgment that nationalizing the governance of commerce would help protect property and economic liberties from the factions and oppressive tendencies of state legislatures.[111]

The privileges and immunities clause in Article IV, section 2, states, "The Citizens of each State shall be entitled to all Privileges and Immunities of Citizens in the several States." This clause has been taken to limit the ways in which states may discriminate against economic interests in other states. The Court recently struck down, for example, a New Hampshire rule limiting bar admissions to lawyers residing in the state. Citizens of one state, the Court affirmed, may not be prevented from doing business in another state on "terms of substantial equality with the citizens of that State."[112]

---

[110]See *Gibbons* v. *Ogden*, 9 Wheat. 1 (1824); and *Cooley* v. *Board of Wardens of the Port of Philadelphia*, 12 How. 299 (1851).

[111]See the *Federalist*, no. 9 and no. 10.

[112]*Supreme Court of New Hampshire* v. *Piper*, 470 U.S. 274 (1985), at 280, quoting *Toomer* v. *Witsell*, 334 U.S. 385, at 396.

Since the downfall of the old substantive due process of the *Lochner*-era Court, Congress's power and discretion under the commerce clause have come to be regarded as extremely broad.[113] Recently, however, the Court established a new limit to the sorts of commercial policies Congress may pursue: the equal protection clause. Congress itself has exempted the states from commerce clause restrictions with regard to the insurance industry, but in *Metropolitan Life Ins. Co. v. Ward,* the Court struck down an Alabama tax preference scheme favoring the state's own insurance companies.[114] The Court held, in effect, that even when the states and Congress act in unison, the equal protection clause of the Fourteenth Amendment limits the permissible types of economic discrimination between a state's residents and nonresidents.

In *Metropolitan Life,* the Court announced that the equal protection clause serves as a bar to economic parochialism and hence to at least some forms of economic as well as racial and other forms of discrimination. The Court majority found the Alabama preference scheme "purely and completely discriminatory" and "the very sort of parochial discrimination that the Equal Protection Clause was intended to prevent."[115] Promoting a national economic union is, the Court seemed to hold, an economic policy choice made by the Constitution for both the states and Congress. The same can be said for the Constitution's commitment to economic rights.

Metropolitan Life drew a dissent uniting proponents of New Right judicial restraint (Justices O'Connor and Rehnquist) with selective activists of the left (Justices Brennan and Marshall). Describing the majority's decision as "astonishing" and "ominous," the dissenters objected to subjecting economic regulation to any meaningful equal protection scrutiny:

The dangers in discerning in the Equal Protection Clause a

[113]See pp. 44–45 above, and *U.S. v. Darby*, 312 U.S. 100 (1941).
[114]470 U.S. 869 (1985).
[115]Ibid., p. 878.

prohibition against barriers to interstate business irrespective of the Commerce Clause should be self-evident. The Commerce Clause is a flexible tool of economic policy that Congress may use as it sees fit, letting it lie dormant or invoking it to limit as well as promote the free flow of commerce. . . . [T]he Court today indicates the Equal Protection Clause stands as an independent barrier if courts should determine that either Congress or a State has ventured in the "wrong" direction. . . . Nothing in the Constitution or our past decisions supports forcing such an economic straightjacket [sic] on the federal system.[116]

But if we put aside the practice of blind deference to government restrictions on economic liberty, there is, contrary to the dissenters in *Metropolitan Life,* no reason why the equal protection clause should not be interpreted as having an economic component. The Court has often taken the promotion of free trade among the states to be one of the central purposes of the Constitution. It is a purpose supported by the privileges and immunities clause, and it has proved to be a means to the preamble's broad goals of forming "a more perfect Union," promoting "the general Welfare," and securing "the Blessings of Liberty." Promotion of a free national economic union, therefore, should be counted among the *ends* sought by the Constitution, and those ends should control our interpretation of constitutional *means,* such as Congress's power to regulate commerce. Given that people have an interest in economic liberty supported by the Constitution, there is every reason to applaud the Court majority in *Metropolitan Life* for helping to reinvigorate judicial scrutiny of economic regulation.

Another harbinger of principled activism was the Court's recent move to infuse a measure of substantive bite into the minimal rationality test. Applying only the minimal review standard, the Court, in *City of Cleburne* v. *Cleburne Living Center,* struck down a

[116]Ibid., p. 901.

municipal ordinance requiring special permits for the establishment of homes for the mentally retarded.[117] Instead of helping the government manufacture pretextual and hypothetical reasons for regulation, as the Court often does in matters not held to involve an arbitrary class of "fundamental rights," the Court critically examined the reasons offered by the city council. The Court found the council's arguments specious and charged that requiring a special permit only for housing for the retarded appeared to rest "on an irrational prejudice against the mentally retarded."[118]

> [M]ere negative attitudes, or fear, unsubstantiated by factors which are properly cognizable in a zoning proceeding, are not permissible bases for treating a home for the mentally retarded differently from apartment houses, multiple dwellings, and the like. . . . "Private biases may be outside the reach of the law, but the law cannot, directly or indirectly, give them effect."[119]

In his concurring opinion in *Cleburne*, Justice Stevens argued that the equal protection clause should be interpreted as imposing a duty on legislators always "to govern impartially." This duty to govern impartially or reasonably embodies the core values of constitutionalism: to have a government of laws rather than of men is to have government based on reasons that *all* ought to be able to accept. Therefore, Stevens objected, "I cannot believe that a rational member of this disadvantaged class could ever approve of the discriminatory application of the city's ordinance in this

[117]473 U.S. 432 (1985). For a harbinger of the beefed-up minimal rationality standard, see *Plyler* v. *Doe*, 457 U.S. 202, 224 (1984). *Plyler* concerned a Texas law denying free public education to the children of illegal aliens. The Court held that although alien children are not a "suspect" class and the right to education is not "fundamental," nevertheless, the challenged classification "can hardly be considered rational unless it furthers some substantial goal of the state" (*Plyler*, p. 224).

[118]*Cleburne*, p. 450.

[119]Ibid., p. 448. The quote is from *Palmore* v. *Sidoti*, 104 S.Ct. 1879 (1984).

case."[120] In effect, Stevens argued that justices must put themselves in the shoes of those being discriminated against and ask themselves whether a special restriction or burden could be judged reasonable. To adopt the perspective of the victim of discrimination is to insist that laws be made on the basis of reasons that can be shared by both the politically powerless and the strong.

Steven's concurring opinion in *Cleburne* adopted precisely the right moral perspective; he demanded that legislators always act as principled expositors of the Constitution. A critical standard of reasonableness ought to be applied to all cases, whether involving civil rights, economic regulation, or any other issue. His defense of judicial scrutiny on equal protection grounds across the whole range of possible challenges to state laws is an important step toward principled activism.[121]

Justices Marshall, Brennan, and Blackmun fully appreciated the import of the strengthened rationality test as applied in *Cleburne*: "The rational basis test invoked today is most assuredly not the rational basis test of Williamson v. Lee Optical. . . . In normal circumstances, the burden is not on the legislature to convince the Court that the lines it has drawn are sensible."[122] Nothing could better sum up the paltriness of the usual minimal review standard than Marshall's admission that it sanctioned laws not shown by the legislature to be "sensible." Marshall's fear was precisely that giving added weight to the minimal review standard opened the way to principled activism, that is, careful review of the reasons advanced to support restrictions on economic, civil, and political freedoms. *Cleburne's* review standard "creates precedent," Marshall said, "for this Court and lower courts to subject economic and commercial classifications to similar and searching 'ordinary' rational basis review—a small and regrettable step back toward the days of Lochner v. New York."[123]

[120]Ibid., p. 455.
[121]See also Stevens's opinion in *Craig* v. *Boren*, 429 U.S. 190 (1976).
[122]*Cleburne*, pp. 458–59.
[123]Ibid., pp. 459–60.

Marshall correctly gauged the implications of *Cleburne*, but the Court should embrace these implications, not reject them. Economic liberty is a constitutional value, and property rights have a place in and deserve some weight in deliberations upon hard questions of constitutional interpretation. This does not mean that laissez-faire must always triumph over competing values, such as Congress's need for discretion in making policy respecting commercial matters. Conscientious adjudicators, however, must not mark off the economic realm as the no-man's-land of unreasonableness, a domain of total and unfettered legislative discretion. The burden of justifying restrictions on economic liberty should rest on legislatures. Moreover, the justifications offered by legislators should be scrutinized by conscientious adjudicators to ensure that legislatures' arguments for economic regulation have adequate empirical support. Anything less invites the whim, pretext, and blatant parochialisim that have degraded our constitutional performance in the economic area.

An important set of values sustains the judiciary's determination to review critically the reasons supporting restrictions on the entire range of liberties with which the Constitution is concerned. Economic liberties, however, are not the only ones threatened by the judiciary's refusal to engage in critical examinations of legislative reasons and evidence.

The final case to be examined concerns the scope of the constitutional right to privacy. This case dramatically illustrates the failures of the minimal rationality standard of review and, more broadly, of New Right jurisprudence. This case also illustrates the inescapable role of moral theory in deciding the proper scope and weight of constitutional rights, whether to property or privacy.

Bowers v. *Hardwick* involved a challenge by a homosexual (Michael Hardwick) to a Georgia law making sodomy a felony.[124] Hardwick

[124]106 S. Ct. 2841 (1986). The case was heard on a motion to dismiss for failure to state a claim. The federal district court dismissed the case for failure to state a claim, but the court of appeals reversed, holding that the Georgia statute violated the fundamental rights of Hardwick.

challenged the statute as a violation of his constitutional right to privacy. By a 5–4 vote, the Supreme Court turned away Hardwick's challenge and denied that the Constitution confers a right to homosexuals to engage in sodomy at home.

The *Hardwick* case falls in the line of cases that began with *Griswold* v. *Connecticut* in which the Court struck down a state law making it a crime for married couples to use contraceptives.[125] *Griswold* established a right to privacy implicit in the broad guarantees of the Constitution, and in doing so the Court revitalized the idea that the Fourteenth Amendment's due process clause implies broad and substantive limitations on the restrictions states may impose upon personal freedom.

In cases after *Griswold*, the Court banned prosecution for possessing obscene materials in the home, and later overturned a conviction under a state law banning distribution of contraceptives to an unmarried person.[126] In these two cases, the constitutional right to privacy was extended from the use of contraceptives by married couples to unmarried couples, and to reading pornography at home. "If the right to privacy means anything," Justice Brennan said, "it is the right of the *individual*, married or single, to be free from unwarranted governmental intrusion into matters so fundamentally affecting a person as the decision whether to beget a child."[127] Against this background—a privacy right of expanding but uncertain limits—the Court decided *Bowers* v. *Hardwick*.

Hardwick is a difficult case; the language of the Constitution, precedent, and historical practice do not, as I shall argue, furnish obvious answers to the questions raised by this case. The Court's

[125]See p. 52 above.

[126]*Eisenstadt* v. *Baird,* 405 U.S. 438 (1972); *Stanley* v. *Georgia,* 394 U.S. 557 (1969).

[127]*Eisenstadt* v. *Baird.* Another case extending the right to privacy was *Roe* v. *Wade,* 410 U.S. 113 (1973), in which Justice Blackmun argued that "[T]his right of privacy . . . is broad enough to encompass a woman's decision whether or not to terminate her pregnancy." *Roe* also raises the distinct and vexing issue of when life begins. Accepting the right to privacy does not necessarily commit one to the decision in *Roe*.

majority, led by Justice White, narrowly interpreted the privacy right as protecting intimate decisions connected with family, marriage, and procreation but not homosexuality. The dissenters, led by Justice Blackmun, interpreted the privacy right as a broad guarantee of protection for personal autonomy and diversity extending to both homosexuals and heterosexuals, that is, not only to traditional family patterns but also to the right to be different.

Although *Hardwick* is a hard case, it has, like most other hard cases, a correct answer, one that turns on a moral judgment: which interpretation of the privacy right constitutes a better vision of what America stands for? Besides dramatizing the inadequacy of the minimal review standard, *Bowers* v. *Hardwick* illustrates the inescapability of moral judgment in constitutional interpretation and, thereby, the emptiness of New Right jurisprudence.

Justice White's opinion for the Court, as noted above, narrowly interpreted the privacy right established before *Hardwick* by construing that right as extending only to matters involving "family, marriage, and procreation." "None of the rights announced in [the previous] cases," said White,

> bears any resemblance to the claimed constitutional right of homosexuals to engage in sodomy. . . . No connection between family, marriage, or procreation on the one hand and homosexual activity on the other has been demonstrated. . . . [T]he proposition that any kind of private sexual conduct between consenting adults is constitutionally insulated from state proscription is unsupportable.[128]

Is this the best reading of the principle established in those previous cases? How do we decide?

White's opinion bears all the distinguishing marks of New Right jurisprudence. He is defensive about the power of the Court in a democracy and advocates a modest role for the judiciary.

---

[128]*Hardwick*, p. 2844.

Judges, White declares, must stick close to the "language and design" of the Constitution: there "should be . . . great resistance to expand the substantive reach of those [due process] Clauses, particularly if it involves redefining the category of rights deemed to be fundamental." He is skeptical concerning judicially enforced constitutional rights because he views judicial power against the background of a basically majoritarian Constitution. The judiciary, he says, must not take "to itself further authority to govern the country without *express* constitutional authority" [emphasis added].[129]

The problem for White's argument is that the Constitution is not basically democratic, and judicial power is not anomalous. The Court is an integral part of a scheme of constitutionally limited government. Judicial power, viewed against the background of constitutionally limited government, is in no way anomalous or in need of special controls. White's exclusive emphasis on "express" rights, moreover, violates the "express" terms of the Ninth Amendment.

By gesturing toward the authority of Original Intent, White's opinion also relies upon a second pillar of New Right jurisprudence. Sodomy, he points out, was a common-law crime in the 13 original colonies, and criminal sodomy statutes were in force in 32 of the 37 states in the Union when the Fourteenth Amendment was ratified.[130]

Once again, White's observations suffer from the weaknesses of an infirm jurisprudence. We know that the framers of the Fourteenth Amendment, for example, positively intended *not* to desegregate public schools, and yet the Court did not let that stand in the way of *Brown* v. *Board of Education*.[131] And quite rightly, too. The framers of the Fourteenth Amendment wrote, and the ratifiers accepted, language requiring that the federal

[129]Ibid., p. 2846.
[130]Ibid., p. 2844–45.
[131]347 U.S. 483 (1954). See Berger, chap. 7.

government guarantee "the equal protection of the laws." Whatever the force of the apparent racial prejudice of the amendment's framers, they did not write that prejudice into law. They wrote a broadly worded amendment, leaving it to future interpreters to flesh out in light of the rest of the constitution and our own best sense of what "equal protection of the laws" requires. White's intentionalism, like all intentionalism, is deployed as a means of fleeing the hard moral judgments required by the words actually adopted and written into law. New Right intentionalism yields a result as iniquitous in *Hardwick* as it would have, if allowed to work, in *Brown*.

White's opinion, finally, relies upon a third pillar of New Right jurisprudence: a broad skepticism about the relevance of moral principles in constitutional interpretation. This skepticism is enunciated most clearly by the Court's unwillingness in *Bowers* to attempt a principled case distinguishing privacy rights associated with family life from those claimed by homosexuals.

White argues that in previous cases the Court extended privacy protections only to decisions involving family relationships, marriage, and procreation. Such fundamental rights as privacy (rights not explicit in the Constitution's text), says White, must be "implicit in the concept of ordered liberty" or "deeply rooted in this Nation's history or tradition." So family and tradition, on Justice White's reading, stand on the side of contracepted and extramarital sex, aborted pregnancies, and pornography—a fairly liberal view of the traditional family.

White concludes, "To claim that a right to engage in such conduct (namely sodomy) is 'deeply rooted in this nation's history or tradition' or 'implicit in the concept of ordered liberty' is, at best, facetious."[132] Is it, however, more facetious than Justice White's artful reading of our "tradition"? Adding unfairness to injustice, White simply tailors our tradition to fit the cases he wishes to distinguish.

[132]*Hardwick*, p. 2846.

71

Because homosexuals have no fundamental right to privacy, according to White, the Georgia statute need only pass the minimal constitutional test, the nonreview standard of the rational basis test. White therefore did not go on to examine critically Georgia's reasons for making homosexual sodomy a felony by seeking evidence of a substantial relation between the statute and a legitimate state purpose. An adequate basis for the law is found, he wrote, in "the *presumed* belief of a majority of the electorate in Georgia that homosexual sodomy is immoral and unacceptable [emphasis added]," and in presumed "majority sentiments about the morality of homosexuality."[133] To presume beliefs or hypothesize legislative reasons where none have been offered is to fling open the door to arbitrary power, contrary to the constitutionalist view that the burden of justifying infringements on liberty should always be on legislators. White's presumption in this case has, moreover, no basis in any legislative act, since the statute in question speaks only of sodomy and not of homosexual sodomy.

Missing from the majority opinions in *Hardwick* was any semblance of critical judgment about the strength of the reasons for banning sodomy. This, too, reveals the Court's moral skepticism in *Hardwick*. Instead of examining the reasons for banning sodomy per se or discussing sexual morality in a way that distinguishes homosexuality, both Justice White and Chief Justice Burger (in a concurring opinion) simply accepted as adequate justification the "ancient roots" of proscriptions on homosexuality. "Decisions of individuals relating to homosexual conduct," wrote Burger, "have been subject to state intervention throughout the history of Western Civilization. Condemnation of those practices is firmly rooted in Judeo-Christian moral and ethical standards."

Burger argued that to claim "that the act of homosexual sodomy is somehow protected as a fundamental right would be to cast aside millennia of moral teaching." But the former chief justice got his history wrong on several counts: homosexuality has been

[133]Ibid., p. 2846.

subject to active state intervention only since the latter half of the 12th century. It was not only tolerated but was accepted as natural by the classical Greeks; it was accepted by the Romans of the Republic and in the Empire until the beginning of its decline in the 3rd century.[134] The moral status of homosexual conduct is, nowadays, not settled but a matter of dispute among theologians.

More important, both Burger and White fail to see that gesturing toward what no one disputes—that homosexuals have often been subject to discrimination and prejudice—does not constitute a reason for perpetuating discrimination. The Court's historical references could count as reasons for continuing to discriminate only if we assume that all historical practices are good, and that assumption is, of course, ludicrous. Prejudices against blacks, Jews, women, and many other groups have "ancient roots." A moment's reflection on the sad but obvious fact that prejudices often persist suffices to show that history cannot be simplistically relied upon in the way the Court did in *Hardwick*. To recommend or condemn a practice, one must justify its reasonableness or goodness; merely referring to "ages of moral teaching" is beside the point.[135]

Furthermore, Burger and White assume that merely pointing to past historical practices is sufficient to locate the American *tradition*. Both justices give the misleading appearance of having morality on their side by confusing two separate ideas: history and tradition. History is simply the record of what has happened, some of it good, some bad. Our history includes lynchings and other manifestations of racism, antisemitism, sexism, and many other forms of intolerance and prejudice. Locating a practice in

[134]John Boswell, *Christianity, Social Tolerance, and Homosexuality* (Chicago: University of Chicago: 1981), p. 71 and passim. Chief Justice Burger's main historical support comes from D. Bailey, *Homosexuality and the Western Christian Tradition* (London: Longmans, Green, 1955), which Boswell supersedes.

[135]It is worth noting again that Justice Stevens has recognized that principled constitutional interpretation requires rising above "stereotyped thinking," which often relies on mere prejudice, on "habit rather than analysis" or reflection. See *Mathews* v. *Lucas*, 427 U.S. 495 (1976), in his dissenting opinion on p. 520.

our history, therefore, does not establish its moral value. Locating a practice in our tradition is something altogether different. To discern a nation's tradition one must articulate and apply moral judgments about what we find valuable, what is worth continuing, what we stand for at our best. A tradition represents a distillation of valuable practices from their suspension in a history that includes actions and events we wish to rise above. Our history is what has happened to us and what we have done. Our tradition is our reflective judgment about what we stand for at our best, what we aspire to.[136]

Practices that provide good ways to go forward, then, are not all of those found in our history, but only those located in our tradition. A tradition cannot be discerned without the aid of moral principles distinguishing valuable from vicious practices. Only by bringing principle to bear on history can we discern a tradition, a justifiable way of going forward, a reason for decisions. By confusing history and tradition, the Court in *Hardwick* simply failed to see the inescapability of moral argument. The reliance on mere history is exactly what one would expect from an uncritical application of the minimal rationality test. The Court failed in *Hardwick* to provide reasons justifying its refusal to recognize an important constitutional right to personal privacy.

Suppose we took the opinions of White and Burger as statements about what America stands for. They imply that at our best we are intolerant and mistrustful, that we act on sentiments and feelings rather than reasons, that we fear that the effort to rise above prejudice will dissolve the fragile and unreasoned bonds holding society together. Such attitudes foster application of the minimal rationality standard of constitutional review, which, as we have seen, stands for no review at all. Moreover, such attitudes nurture the anxious fear that our politics is held together by no more than prejudice, sentiment, and belief. These attitudes represent the antithesis of that appropriate to constitutionalists,

---

[136]This distinction is developed in Barber, pp. 84–85.

to those determined to honor the rule of law, the rule of impartial reasoning. Can we do better?

The infirmities of the majority opinions in *Hardwick*—their reliance on a misleadingly simple concept of constitutional democracy, their pointless invocation of Original Intent, and their confused flight from moral judgment—exemplify the infirmities of the New Right's jurisprudence. Fortunately, the minority opinions in *Hardwick* point in the direction of something better, something closer to a principled activism on behalf of individual liberty.

Justice Blackmun's dissenting opinion characterized the right at stake in *Hardwick* more generally and more abstractly than did the majority's. The case, he said, is not about sodomy but about the "right to be let alone." The Court's finding, he claimed, rested on nothing more than the history of prejudice, on the mere fact that "many states . . . still make such conduct illegal and have done so for a very long time."[137]

The core of the state's defense of its ban on sodomy is, Blackmun noted, that homosexuals interfere with Georgia's exercise of its right to maintain a decent society. Furthermore, Georgia's only justification for the ascription of indecency to homosexuality is the assertion that these acts have been "uniformly condemned" for hundreds if not thousands of years.[138] "It is revolting," said Blackmun (quoting Holmes), "to have no better reason for a rule of law than that so it was first laid down in the time of Henry IV. It is still more revolting if the grounds upon which it was laid down have vanished long since, and the rule simply persists from blind imitation of the past." If constitutional rights stand for anything, Blackmun contended, they "must mean that, before Georgia can prosecute its citizens for making choices about the most intimate aspects of their lives, it must do more than assert

---

[137]*Hardwick*, p. 2848, quoting p. 2843.
[138]Ibid., p. 2854.

that the choice they have made is . . . an 'abominable crime not fit to be named among Christians.' "[139]

Blackmun rejected the majority's reliance on mere historical persistence: "I cannot agree that either the length of time a majority has held its convictions or the passions with which it defends them can withdraw legislation from the Court's scrutiny."[140] He realized, furthermore, that the partisan reasons of particular religious groups cannot, as such, count as legitimate, impartial reasons for secular legislation. Some religions regard homosexuality as sinful, but that "gives the state no license to impose" these judgments on the whole polity:

> The legitimacy of secular legislation depends instead on whether the State can advance some justification for its law beyond its conformity to religious doctrine. . . . A state can no more punish private behavior because of religious intolerance than it can punish such behavior because of racial animus.[141]

As Justice Stevens insisted in *Cleburne*, only impartial reasons, reasons that *all* ought to be able to accept, can count as good reasons in constitutional interpretation. Religiously grounded intolerance, historically persistent practices of prejudice and discrimination, and simple feelings of disapproval—none of these can be invoked to support state infringements on individual liberty.

At our best, Blackmun's argument implies, we strive to rise above unreasonable feelings, habits, and prejudices. Americans aspire, on this reading, to be governed by reasons and to protect the victims of discrimination and prejudice.

To show how his broader construction of the privacy right is rooted in America's tradition of solicitude for the powerless,

[139]Ibid., p. 2848.
[140]Ibid., p. 2854.
[141]Ibid., p. 2854–55.

Blackmun invoked certain cases in which the Court interceded on behalf of victims of prejudice. In *West Virginia School Board* v. *Barnette*, for example, the Court intervened on behalf of the children of Jehovah's Witnesses who were expelled from public school when they refused on religious grounds to salute the flag.[142] In that case, Justice Robert H. Jackson wrote:

> We apply the limitations of the Constitution with no fear that freedom to be intellectually and spiritually diverse or even contrary, will disintegrate the social organization. . . . [F]reedom to differ is not limited to things that do not matter much. That would be a mere shadow of freedom. The test of its substance is the right to differ as to things that touch the heart of the existing order.[143]

Besides linking the judicial enforcement of a right to personal privacy with an American tradition of protection for minorities, Blackmun also enunciated a principled explanation of why the values underlying the previous privacy rights cases justified protections for homosexuals as well. Why, Blackmun asked, have we protected family privacy? We protect rights not in order to promote public welfare or to preserve traditional patterns of life, but because intimate associations and choices "form a central part in an individual's life."[144] "The concept of privacy," he maintained, "embodies the 'moral fact that a person belongs to himself and not to others or to society as a whole.' " The values at stake

[142]319 U.S. 624, 641–42 (1943).

[143]Other cases Blackmun relied upon include *Wisconsin* v. *Yoder*, 406 U.S. 205 (1972), protecting the right of the Amish to withdraw their children from public school; and *Loving* v. *Virginia*, 388 U.S. 1 (1967), striking down a state miscegenation statute. Justice Stevens's dissenting opinion in *Bowers* invoked *Loving* to support his claim that historical belief of the governing majority about immorality of a practice is insufficient reason for upholding a statute. For Stevens, the individual interest in privacy is supported by an even more basic value rooted in our nation's history and tradition: the "individual's right to make certain unusually important decisions that will affect his own, or his family's destiny. . . . [T]he citizen's right to decide how to live his own life" (*Hardwick*, p. 2858).

[144]*Hardwick*, p. 2851.

in previous privacy cases, he implied, are moral and individualistic. Freedom in our intimate associations with others provides the "ability independently to define one's identity," and "is central to any concept of liberty."[145]

Blackmun went on to link personal privacy with economic rights. Previous privacy cases, Blackmun continued, protect not only certain intimate choices but also certain places. The privacy of intimate association in the home implies a more general right of privacy associated with home ownership. The Fourth Amendment's protection of "the right of people to be secure in their . . . houses" is the most explicit of the various provisions supporting the privacy right found in *Griswold*. The liberty of consenting adults to engage in intimate relations at home is, Blackmun argued, at the very heart of the privacy right articulated in earlier cases, and so the right claimed by Hardwick is indeed justified.

The moral thrust of Blackmun's argument is captured succinctly by David Richards:

> The attempt by law to isolate and criminally condemn such forms of sexual expression [as homosexuality] works a kind of spiritual violence on the moral integrity of many persons for whom such acts authenticate the affection, and the mutual love integral to their conceptions of life lived well and humanely. On examination, this brutal and callous impersonal manipulation by the state of intimate personal life is the same constitutional evil as that condemned by the Supreme Court in disallowing the legitimacy of state control of contraceptive use in sexuality or state control of women's use of their bodies for procreation. Such coercive laws must satisfy a heavy burden of constitutional justification; they cannot do so.[146]

Care, commitment, intimate society, free self-definition, the

---

[145]Ibid.

[146]David A. J. Richards, *Toleration and the Constitution* (New York: Oxford University Press, 1986), p. 272.

78

security of the home—all of these values and more are promoted through homosexual as well as heterosexual relationships, and so, Blackmun argued, the Court badly misunderstood the liberty interests at stake in *Hardwick*. It failed to recognize that a proper interpretation of the principles underlying previous privacy cases does justify a right to privacy for homosexuals.

Blackmun's dissenting opinion in *Hardwick* implies a vision of what America stands for that differs sharply from the one offered by the Court's majority. As Blackmun suggested, the moral core of America's constitutional aspirations consists of our striving to be governed by impartial reasons, a resolve to protect the victims of prejudice, and a recognition that freedom leads naturally to a diversity that should be tolerated, not suppressed.[147]

Bowers v. *Hardwick* poses hard questions for constitutionalists: which values have pride of place in the Constitution's scheme of values; which are most deeply rooted in the nation's tradition? Is the power of the states to enforce dominant feelings about sexual morality and "decency" consistent with protections for family freedom, liberally understood? Or does a broader privacy right, based on tolerance of individual freedom and diversity, apply? What sort of freedom and privacy does America stand for?

These questions cannot, as I have argued, be answered by reference to the words of the Constitution, past cases, and history alone. This case confronts us with an inescapable necessity for a critical moral judgment about the rights that individuals ought to have against state interference. Only on the basis of a moral judgment can we say which interpretation of case law and history is better. The *Hardwick* case illustrates the truth that constitutional interpreters cannot flee from hard moral judgments; they can either make such judgments and defend them, as Blackmun did, or stumble into them or past them, as did White and Burger.

---

[147]See also *Federalist*, no. 10, where Madison notes that diversity is the natural result of liberty.

Blackmun gives us something wholly lacking in the majority's opinions, a principled argument for deciding a hard case, a case not easily disposed of by the text of the Constitution, by history, or by precedent. Of course, the particular principles Blackmun invokes are disputable, and there is more to be said on both sides of this difficult issue. On the strength of the arguments examined here, however, one must conclude that homosexuals have the right to privacy the Court denied to them. Moreover, the spirit of Blackmun's opinion is precisely what is called for in constitutional interpretation. It reflects a determination to face and make the hard judgments of political morality with which the Constitution confronts us, and that determination in turn rests on an aspiration to be governed by reasons rather than prejudices and feelings.

To view any of the cases examined here as "fringe" cases would be a grave error. The advances made in *Metropolitan Life* and *Cleburne*, and the sorry lapse of the majority opinion in *Hardwick*, are matters that go to the heart of constitutionalism's commitment to reasonableness. Judicial review stands for the peculiar kind of respect that our system of government pays to all citizens who are subject to governmental power—property owners as well as those who are objects of majority prejudice. When judges properly exercise their review power, demanding real reasons and evidence before allowing restrictions on individual liberty, judicial review helps ensure that majorities treat minorities as fellow citizens worthy of being reasoned with.

Judicial review helps create a valuable form of political community. This brings us to the fourth pillar of New Right jurisprudence: the "communitarian" claim that individual rights dissolve the bonds that hold communities together. The question posed by the cases examined here is not whether we are to be a community, but what sort of community we are to be. As with historical practices, so too with communities; not all are valuable. Some communities are held together by prejudice or mere feelings, and some are sustained by fear and suspicion of "outsiders"

80

or those who are different. Such a vision of community often seems to underlie the jurisprudence of the New Right.

Principled activism offers not an abandonment of community in favor of solitary individualism but a critical judgment about which communities are valuable. Those sustained by hate, fear, ignorance, and prejudice are not worth preserving. Americans can do better. According to principled activism, the Constitution creates and judicial review supports a political community held together by reasoned self-government, a community of citizens capable of treating each other reasonably.

Principled activism helps create a community of principle not only by empowering the judiciary. Principled activism stands for the idea, as Justice Stevens suggested in *Cleburne,* that legislators have a *pervasive* duty always to act on good reasons, to offer sound constitutional reasons for all restrictions on liberties. This broad duty is itself supported by the Constitution's concern with a broad range of economic and human rights. To exempt state legislators from the duty to justify restrictions on economic liberty or the privacy of disfavored groups is inconsistent with a conscientious desire to apply and enforce the Constitution's own values.

We need, therefore, to revise our understanding of the workings of the courts and the political process itself. One argument often put forward in defense of the double standard in constitutional law, for example, is that political and regulatory processes, without meaningful judicial review, can be trusted to produce equitable economic arrangements. Such a claim cannot withstand scrutiny.

Selective activists on the left rightly believe that a long tradition of racial prejudice provides a strong justification for their suspicion of laws relying, explicitly or implicitly, on racial distinctions. But in elections and the policymaking process, corrupt economic incentives often are at work. Benefits derived from government programs or regulations are often confined to a few individuals or groups, whereas their costs can be dispersed over millions of taxpayers or consumers who scarcely notice. Exclusionary zoning laws, regulations that disadvantage some competitors, and licensing requirements that keep potential competitors out of a market are but a few examples.[148] Politics presents innumerable opportunities for the pursuit of private interests at the expense of other people.

It may be that laws resting on racial classifications, to take one example, do merit greater judicial scrutiny than economic regulations. Prejudice is a motive for legislation that renders the political process corrupt and illegitimate. Nevertheless, pursuit of mere personal gain at the expense of others is also a corrupt motive.[149] Political regulation of economic affairs manifests its own forms of injustice and corruption. There are solid background reasons, then, for a healthy judicial suspicion about economic legislation, especially that which places burdens on particular individuals or economic groups.

The effective nonreview of economic legislation at work in the minimum rationality standard as applied flies in the face of our knowledge about politics. The nonreview of cases involving economic liberty is an unconstitutional standard of inquiry for another reason as well. The notion that the Constitution speaks only to political and civil rights and not to economic liberty cannot withstand even a cursory reading of the founding document. The Constitution protects individual liberty in general, and that is not hard to explain or justify. Free economic activity not only sustains a productive society and provides outlets for human energy and creativity, it also allows people to build and preserve spheres of

---

[148]For an excellent recent study of the misuse of licensing laws, see S. David Young, *The Rule of Experts* (Washington: Cato Institute, 1987). Gabriel Kolko's study of the private interests behind the rise of business regulation is still a classic; see *The Triumph of Conservatism* (New York: Free Press, 1963).

[149]I am, obviously, taking issue here with much recent democratic theory that regards the pursuit of personal gain as an acceptable engine of electoral competition. My argument is more fully developed in *Liberal Virtues: A Liberal Theory of Citizenship, Virtue, and Community* (Oxford: Oxford University Press, forthcoming).

autonomy and personal security that are supportive of all other liberties.

Vocations, professions, and even common trades and occupations represent more than an investment of time and effort. They are choices of ways of life. Our occupations often shape our identities as deeply as what we read or learn through the news media, as deeply as the intimate choices we make. And economic liberty is bound up with personal security as well as personal liberty and self-definition. The security of the home and personal effects protects not only privacy or "property" but an investment of time and care spent in fashioning a particular way of life. The home shields our intimate association with others and, like our occupations, shapes us as we shape them.

Property rights and economic liberties, of course, converge with other personal values, such as the security of the home, the survival of valued communities and associations, and the maintenance of freely chosen ways of life. The claim of principled activism is that judges should critically review the reasons put forward for economic regulations and, further, that the value of economic liberty and private property must be allowed its due weight in the admittedly difficult process of evaluating competing constitutional values.

Economic security and property rights shield some of the deepest and most valuable aspects of free human existence. Judges might, therefore, start by scrutinizing legislation touching on those forms of free economic activity and property ownership most closely related to liberties already being protected. The right to engage in an occupation and the security of the home would be good places to begin. Such economic rights merit judicial scrutiny for many of the same reasons that other "personal" rights (such as privacy) do.[150] But even those economic activities not so closely connected with personal life and individual auton-

---

[150]Judges should begin, that is, by overturning such decisions as *Wickard, Poletown,* and *Lee Optical;* see pp. 51–52 and 57 above.

omy deserve judicial protection because the Constitution supports free-market values and because corrupt motives of self-interest are at work in political activities concerned with all economic matters.

Admittedly, principled activism goes against the grain of certain cherished myths. Since Holmes's *Lochner* dissent, intellectual dogma has held that the Court should be indifferent about whether a legislature, as Justice Black said, "takes for its textbook Adam Smith, Herbert Spencer, Lord Keynes, or some other."[151] Legal and popular dogma has held that the Constitution represents a choice of certain "political" values (values concerning the democratic process and various political and civil rights), but that it leaves economic policy entirely to the unfettered choice of elected officials. It is as though the choice of economic theory—whether Smith, Keynes, or even Marx—is supremely indifferent so far as the Constitution is concerned. Such a position is untenable. This stark double standard flies in the face of constitutional text and tradition, neglects the fact that many economic and personal liberties are closely interrelated, and ignores the pervasive duty to govern reasonably.

I am not arguing that we must leap boldly back to the *Lochner* era, immediately invalidating the welfare state as unconstitutional. The value of economic liberty (even when politically contested), however, cannot be ignored by constitutional interpreters any more than the value of free speech can be ignored because some think it dangerous. The shape and nature of First Amendment rights depend upon contestable arguments about the intrinsic importance of free speech to human life and its consequences for society. Economic liberties raise similarly tough issues, and these also must be addressed by conscientious adjudicators. In neither instance should concern for liberty be left entirely to legislators.

Some people fear that constitutionalizing economic issues would

[151]*Ferguson* v. *Skrupka*, 372 U.S. 726 (1963).

make the Constitution a "partisan" document. But the Constitution already is and must be a partisan document. It stands for certain values and excludes competing values; it makes important choices. The issue is not partisanship per se, but what form of partisanship informs the most defensible interpretation of the founding document. My claim is that conscientious interpreters should be partisans of principled activism.

One might be excused for believing, in any case, that the polity would be better off with a more politicized Constitution. The most striking feature of the Constitution's bicentennial celebrations has been the utterly platitudinous nature of discussions about the founding document. Our polity seems to have drifted so far from its constitutional roots that we have lost the ability even to speak in constitutional terms, much less to understand what the Constitution stands for. Viewing the whole of politics, including the economic realm, through constitutional lenses is one way of reinvigorating constitutional debate.

Improving the level of public constitutional debate is crucial for the vitality of the founding document. Only when citizens themselves insist that not only Supreme Court justices but also elected officials take the Constitution seriously will we recover from our pathetic condition of constitutional amnesia. Until citizens insist that the Constitution matters in politics, that is, until we politicize the Constitution and thereby constitutionalize our politics, that hallowed document will become more and more a dead letter, revered in its political vacuity. The path to recovery is illuminated by cases such as *Metropolitan Life* and *Cleburne* and by the dissenting opinions in *Bowers* v. *Hardwick*.

One final New Right challenge to an individual rights-centered jurisprudence remains to be taken up: consideration of the claim that a polity that gives its highest allegiance to individual rights surrenders to moral relativism and abandons the possibility of realizing in its political practices a form of moral community.

VII. Liberty and Community

The broadly rights-based jurisprudence outlined in the preceding sections is open to an important line of criticism. Bork and other figures of the New Right have put forward a version of what may be called the communitarian critique of liberal politics. Bork claims that judges who actively defend individual rights are moved by "extra-constitutional moral and political notions" to substitute "moral relativism" for a common morality.[152] However, does a central constitutional concern with individual rights represent the abandonment of a common or public morality?

Bork explains his opposition to what he calls the "privatization of morality" in terms that have been repeated and paraphrased by Attorney General Meese:

> As Lord Devlin said, "What makes a society is a community of ideas, not political ideas alone but also ideas about the way its members should behave and govern their lives." A society that ceases to be a community increases the danger that weariness with turmoil and relativism may bring about an order in which many more, and more valuable, freedoms are lost than those we thought we were protecting.[153]

Terry Eastland, special assistant to Meese, worries about the triumph of a "culture of rights" in an America

> so awash in rights that we are virtually unable to pass legislation reflecting traditional religious and moral views. Moral relativism will then be the rule, at law; and what is true at

[152]Bork, *Tradition*, p. 3.
[153]Ibid., p. 4; also quoted in part and paraphrased in part by Meese, AEI address, pp. 10–11.

law will shape what is practiced. For when morality is strictly up to the individual, with no judgment possible by communities, it is likely that everyone will do what is right in his own eyes. . . . America will then become a land composed of strangers whose religion, if any, is a private matter, and who are bound by no social ties or common aspirations.[154]

Contrary to the views of "liberal" justices, the New Right would allow legislatures to enforce the majority's view of good conduct in spheres often considered private. Bork rejects the idea that "individuals are entitled to their moral beliefs but may not gather as a community to express those beliefs as law."[155] He would treat violations of the majority's view of good conduct as "moral harms" against the community at large—harms to be treated as "pollution" to the moral "atmosphere." The New Right rejects the old idea that individuals should be free to live as they choose as long as they respect the equal freedom of others. For Bork, the "major freedom, of our kind of society is the freedom to choose to have a public morality."[156]

To shield the power of a moral majority from judicial interventions on behalf of individual rights, Bork distinguishes between what he calls the "common sense of the community," which include its practices and traditions, and "abstract and philosophical" arguments, such as the "universalistic style of legal thought" propounded by "theorists of moral abstraction."[157] Bork wishes to vest political authority in the "common sense of the people," that is, in a common sense untutored by philosophy and unrestrained by reflection. Individual rights, which shield people in their private conduct from the meddling of others, are treated by the New Right as obstacles to the majority's power to impose a single and exacting code of conduct on all.

[154]Terry Eastland, "The Politics of Morality and Religion: A Primer," in *Whose Values?* ed. Carl Horn (Ann Arbor, Mich.: Servant Books, 1985), p. 17.

[155]Bork, *Tradition*, p. 3.

[156]Ibid., p. 9.

[157]Ibid., pp. 7–11.

Just how one would go about reconciling Bork's moral skepticism with his concern to promote a "public morality" is not clear. But neither is it clear, as noted above, how this skepticism can be squared with the apparently principled preference for majoritarianism. (Without a principle of moral equality, why should one prefer the "gratifications" of the majority to those of a minority?) Nor is it at all obvious that the majority's right to rule is any less abstract than the individual rights to liberty that Bork dismisses as "too abstract." To seek logical coherence in Bork's position is fruitless; its coherence is rhetorical rather than logical.

What is clear is that the New Right errs in identifying individual rights with moral relativism. The liberal norms that underlie individual rights embody a public morality, and this liberal public morality comports with the Constitution and tradition and moral reasons more substantial than any advanced by the New Right.

The individual rights-centered public morality has another virtue lacking in the intolerant morality of the New Right: it is morally defensible in a vast, heterogeneous republic such as the United States, in which people differ widely about their religious beliefs, lifestyles, goals, and commitments. The relevant question is not whether America is to be a moral community, but what kind of community it is to be. The important question is whether America should be an open, tolerant community that respects liberty, individuality, and diversity.

The political supremacy of a conception of justice centered on the value of liberty and individual rights forms the core of the tradition of liberal individualism. And the term "liberal" is taken here to refer not to the narrow contemporary sense that marks off the left side of the American political spectrum but to the older and broader sense of the term, represented centrally by such figures as John Locke and John Stuart Mill and the founders of the American republic.[158]

[158]Bork refers dismissively to Mill's classic *On Liberty*. (See Bork, *Tradition*, p. 5.) It should be noted here that liberal thought is now split between adherents to classical liberalism (or libertarianism) and proponents of contemporary (or egalitarian)

To recognize the moral force of individuality is to recognize that intelligent, responsible persons can and do pursue widely divergent personal goals and projects. This observation is especially true in a vast, diverse nation such as the United States. This "extended republic" embraces a vast populace with a dizzying variety of faiths, cultures, goals, and lifestyles. Liberalism stands for the conviction that each person has a basic duty to respect the rights of others. Liberals hold that people derive their common dignity and equal right to liberty not from any particular allegiance to nation, class, sect, or caste, but from their capacity to reflect and understand, to choose and act and be held responsible, to settle on projects and pursue them, to change their minds and begin again, and to restrain their desires and the pursuit of their goals when other people's rights are at stake.

French sociologist Émile Durkheim well understood that liberal individualism represents not the abandonment of public values or of community but the embrace of a substantive moral vision that accords with a people's diversity. It is worth quoting Durkheim at some length.

Doubtless if the dignity of the individual derived from his individual qualities, or from those particular characteristics which distinguish him from others, one might fear that he would become enclosed in a sort of moral egoism that would render all social cohesion impossible. But in reality he receives his dignity from a higher source, one which he shares with all men. . . . It is humanity that is sacred and worthy of respect. And this is not his exclusive possession. It is distributed among his fellows, and in consequence he cannot take

---

liberalism. All liberals share the values being defended in this discussion against Bork's conservatism: the basic right of all persons to choose how to live—to devise, pursue, and revise a plan of life within the bounds set by the equal freedom of others. But the concern with both economic and noneconomic rights is typical only of classical liberalism. Contemporary liberals tend to downgrade economic rights in favor of income redistribution; they support the modern variant of the double standard discussed in chapter 5.

it as a goal for his conduct without being obliged to go beyond himself and turn toward others. . . . Impersonal and anonymous, such an end soars above all particular consciences and can thus serve as a rallying point for them. . . . All that societies require in order to hold together is that their members fix their eyes on the same end and come together in a single faith. . . . [I]ndividualism thus understood is not the glorification of the self, but of the individual in general. Its motive force is not egoism but sympathy for all that is human, a wider pity for all sufferings, for all human miseries, a more ardent desire to combat and alleviate them, a greater thirst for justice. Is this not the way to achieve a community of all men of good will?[159]

Liberal citizens recognize that their rights are grounded in principles and values that protect individualism in general. Liberal principles are based not on self-love but on respect for diversity, plurality, and the dignity of beings with the capacity for reflective and responsible choice. In this way, liberal individualism becomes a moral commitment, a commitment embodying general, impersonal concerns and values that overarch and subordinate self-centeredness. Thus understood, individual liberty provides the foundation for a public morality, a moral community.

The supremacy of the Constitution embodies liberalism's ultimate commitment to moral standards. The Constitution, properly interpreted, embodies not simply the will of some authoritative group but standards of justice and respect for the full gamut of moral rights. Bork, however, would deny this moral status to the Constitution. He continually emphasizes that judges owe their allegiance to the will of the Framers (in the form of specific historical intentions) or to the will of the majority. And in the place of rights, justice, and morality, he believes only in the

[159]Émile Durkheim, "Individualism and the Intellectuals," trans. and intro. Steven Lukes, *Political Studies* 17, no. 1 (1969): 23–24.

gratifications and preferences of the greatest number. This moral cynicism devalues the status of the Constitution and cheapens the currency of our political discourse; it also undermines the possibility of a moral community in America.

It is surely unrealistic to expect that the citizens of this diverse nation will ever settle on a single vision of the good life. We can neither hope nor expect that one such vision will ever secure the allegiance of Jerry Falwell and Jane Fonda, of urban yuppies and suburban families, of Midwestern farmers and Vietnamese immigrants. To grant supreme political status to the preferences of the greatest number, rather than to public moral norms protecting the equal liberty of all, constitutes oppression and invites social conflict.

Individuals prize rights not because they wish to live in isolation but because they want to choose with whom to associate, in what manner, and for what purpose. After all, people's disagreements about personal preferences and lifestyles are as wide and deep as their differences over religious beliefs. To require all to live according to one set of ideals, one vision of the good life, would be to turn back the clock to the era of religious civil wars following the Reformation. It would indeed be ironic if Americans, descendants of those who sought to establish a haven from religious persecution, abandoned liberal toleration, liberal peace, and liberal justice for the spurious traditionalism of the New Right.

Community ends with coercion; it doesn't begin there. And a community cannot be a moral community unless it is also a free community. The rights that define associative freedoms, and those that provide for autonomy and personal security, are part of the constitution of any good community. They are part of what makes community valuable. And so individual rights, far from being corrosive of community as the New Right charges, are constitutive components of America's liberal, constitutional community.

VIII. Conclusion

The central pillars of the jurisprudence of the New Right crumble when subjected to scrutiny. The Jurisprudence of Original Intent raises a host of apparently insoluble problems, and it ends in self-destruction when it becomes evident that the Framers did not intend the republic to be guided by their specific historical intentions. Historical intentions, in any case, are invoked selectively rather than consistently by the conservatives as a means of advancing a majoritarian political program that itself is deeply at odds with the text and spirit of the Constitution, the ideas of the Founders, and much of our political tradition. The New Right's majoritarianism is serviced not only by the selective invocation of original intentions but also by the selective invocation of moral skepticism: the cynical acid that is meant to dissolve "abstract" individual rights is never applied to the majority's purported right to rule. And yet, as pointed out here, unless one inserts an "abstract" premise of moral equality, there is no reason to prefer the gratifications of the majority to those of the minority.

Moral skepticism, like intentionalism and majoritarianism, is more than extraneous to the Constitution; it is positively at odds with the founding document, the Declaration of Independence, the ideas of the Founders, and the moral aspirations of Americans at their best. The New Right fails to recognize, finally, that individual rights are supportive both of community and morality. In dismissing individual liberty and rights as "relativistic" and corrosive of moral community, the New Right undermines the political morality that the Constitution itself embodies.

The jurisprudence of the New Right creates a moral void at the heart of the Constitution. Bork and others see a community concerned with rights as one whose members are drifting apart, growing weary "with turmoil and relativism," and becoming "strangers" to one another.[160] The point of this exercise, for at least some on the New Right, is clear enough. They wish to fill the moral vacuum they establish in liberal constitutionalism with religious values, specifically with Christian values. As Terry Eastland puts it:

> Protestant Christianity . . . tutored the first generations of Americans. It provided what we today would call the value system of the society. . . . Christianity provided an attitude toward law that law itself could not provide. It instilled in Americans the civic virtues of respect for legitimate authority and obedience to it. By strengthening the legal order, Christianity in turn strengthened the social order and thus the bonds of community from which emerge still other civic virtues—those of altruism, neighborliness, and patriotism.[161]

But religion is mentioned only twice in the Constitution. Just before its ratification provisions and signing, the Constitution says that "no religious Test shall ever be required as a Qualification to any Office or public Trust under the United States," and in the opening words of the First Amendment, it says that "Congress shall make no law respecting an establishment of religion, or prohibiting the free exercise thereof." The public morality embodied in the Constitution, while it surely accommodates free religious practice, does not rest on particular religious beliefs or on the presumption of religious agreement.

This essay has tried to suggest that the Constitution should not be read in terms of specific historical intentions, or as the expression of the will of some authoritative group, or as an acknowledgment of majority sovereignty. The Constitution is better read in terms of the aspirations set out in the preamble, as an attempt to, among other things, "establish Justice . . . promote the gen-

---

[160]Bork, *Tradition*, p. 4; Eastland, p. 72.
[161]Eastland, pp. 14–15.

eral Welfare, and secure the Blessings of Liberty to ourselves and our Posterity." The Constitution's aspirations are moral, and, when fleshed out by the interpreter, they are capable of providing the sorts of common values and ideals that may unite even a diverse community.

The ideal of community implicit in the Constitution would count tolerance, openness to change and diversity, and reflectiveness among its public virtues. Furthermore, the very practice of respecting the rights of people who lead different lives fosters liberal attitudes of broad sympathies, friendliness, and even altruism. Citizens loyal to our liberal, democratic Constitution support reasoned public deliberation and persuasion rather than force and arbitrary power. As conscientious interpreters, they would review the acts of public officials for conformity with the Constitution and be prepared to act in politics themselves as pursuers of constitutional ideals and not as promoters of narrow interests.[162]

One would have to be very naive or blind to claim that our current political practices realize this ideal vision of constitutional community. However, this ideal is adumbrated by the Constitution and it is far more attractive than the opposing vision advanced by the New Right. Principled judicial activism would help move us closer to this ideal.

The issues discussed in this essay are "constitutional" in the broadest and deepest sense, affecting not only the determination of court cases but also the shape of our polity and our lives as citizens. In this sense, constitutional interpretation cannot help but be political, and politics, at least at its best, cannot dispense with serious constitutional debate.

The judicial activism defended here should not be confused with judicial supremacy. Principled activism in no way implies that the Supreme Court is the final interpreter of the Constitution

[162]See Stephen Macedo, *Liberal Virtue: A Liberal Theory of Citizenship, Virtue, and Community* (Oxford: Oxford University Press, forthcoming).

(except for the parties to the cases that come before it, and for inferior courts) or that Supreme Court interpretations of the Constitution are binding on Congress, the president, or the citizenry. The Constitution itself is supreme, and the members of each of the three coordinate branches of the federal government are sworn to uphold the Constitution in performing their official functions; the oaths and the coordinate status of the president and members of Congress imply that they have an obligation to interpret for themselves and not to defer to others. As President Andrew Jackson put it, "Each public officer who takes an oath to support the Constitution swears that he will support it as he understands it and not as it is understood by others."[163] Presidents Jefferson and Lincoln also argued, albeit with some variations, for a view of the three branches of the federal government as competing interpreters.[164]

Rejecting the constitutional vision of the New Right should not be confused with a wholesale rejection of conservative sentiments or of patriotism. Only a blind conservatism is without reasons for valuing what it seeks to preserve. Only an unreflective and uncritical patriotism ("my country, right or wrong") forgets that it is in aspiring to worthy principles and ideals that government, Constitution, and country become worthy of loyalty, allegiance, and self-sacrifice. Instead of the unreflective traditionalism of the New Right, we would do far better to aspire to Lincoln's eulogistic remembrance of Henry Clay, who, Lincoln said, "loved his country partly because it was his own country, but mostly because it was a free country; and he burned with a zeal for its advancement . . . because he saw in such, the advancement . . . of human liberty, human right, and human nature."[165]

[163]Andrew Jackson, as quoted in John Agresto, *The Supreme Court and Constitutional Democracy* (Ithaca, N.Y.: Cornell University Press, 1984), p. 128.

[164]Agresto, chap. 5.

[165]Pangle, p. 30.

Postscript: A Debate on Judicial Activism

Stephen Macedo: "The kind of man who demands that govern-ment enforce his ideas," said H. L. Mencken, "is always the kind whose ideas are idiotic."

Mencken's political cynicism is a great temptation, especially when political opinions that we find objectionable are framed as matters of principle, moral claims, or claims of constitutional rights.

But as tempting as cynicism can be, it is of no practical help or guidance. For the fact is—the government *must* enforce *someone's* ideas. And unless there is the possibility that some ideas about politics really are better than others, better in the sense of better justified or truer, then all government rests only on power, or mere "will." If the cynic is correct, there can be no way of distin-guishing between right and wrong, between justice and tyranny, between fidelity to law and willful innovation. To give in to cynicism, then, is to give up on trying to justify our political arrangements. It is to concede that all political arrangements are equally arbitrary, equally unjustified, and distinguishable only in terms of whose ox is being gored.

The jurisprudence of the New Right, at least as articulated by Chief Justice William Rehnquist, Judge Robert Bork, and Attor-ney General Edwin Meese, rests on moral cynicism. Their posi-tion is this: that when activist justices interpret individual rights broadly in the name of principles smacking of "philosophy" or morality, you can be sure that these unelected judges are really

This is the edited transcript of a debate between Stephen Macedo and Gary McDowell, then associate director of public affairs for the U.S. Department of Justice and now resident scholar at the Center for Judicial Studies, held at the Cato Institute on November 20, 1986.

only using the Constitution as a way of imposing their own personal preferences on the community. Judges must stay away from philosophy and morality and stick close to the text, structure, and purpose of the Constitution itself, the Constitution as it was written. And when text, structure, and purpose are unclear, says the New Right, justices must complete the meaning of the text by looking to the specific historical intentions of those who framed or ratified the text in question.

Moved by moral cynicism, the New Right confronts the flawed moral arguments of liberal judicial activists, not by seeking better moral arguments, but by condemning the resort to morality altogether.

The problem faced by the New Right is this: Constitutional text, structure, purpose—and certainly everything we know about the moral confidence of our 18th-century statesmen—all draw conscientious interpreters toward, and not away from, morality. The New Right's advocacy of judicial restraint is not the consequence of taking the Constitution seriously—it is the consequence of ignoring those parts of the Constitution that moral skeptics and majoritarians find inconvenient.

When New Right advocates of judicial restraint tell us that the Constitution's purposes must be located in the particular historical conceptions of the Framers, this is not out of respect for the text, but in place of serious reflection on the purposes that the text itself announces:

> We the People of the United States, in order to form a more perfect union, establish justice, insure domestic tranquility, provide for the common defense, promote the general welfare, and secure the blessings of liberty to ourselves and our posterity, do ordain and establish this Constitution for the United States of America.

These are the purposes that the Constitution itself announces, these are the intentions that count. They are broad moral purposes, consistent with the moral confidence of the Framers. Those who summon up particular historical intentions not stated in the Constitution do so in order to evade the text, not to vindicate it.

And so, Chief Justice Rehnquist, in a speech several years ago debunking what he called the "cliché" that the Constitution "can fairly be described as a charter which guarantees rights to individuals against the government," referred to the "Bill of Rights" as a term "commonly applied to the first eight amendments to the United States Constitution." Of course, every schoolchild knows what the chief justice on this occasion conveniently forgot: that there are 10 amendments in the Bill of Rights, and that the Ninth tells us that individuals have rights not explicitly mentioned in the document itself: "The enumeration in the Constitution, of certain rights, shall not be construed to deny or disparage others retained by the people." The Ninth Amendment, then, like the preamble, is a part of the text that propels the conscientious interpreter beyond the text itself. What other rights do we have? The Constitution doesn't say, but it says we have them, and it says they are *rights,* moral claims not dependent on mere historical circumstance, accident, or will.

Before getting to the need for a morally principled judicial activism, let me briefly address two other shaky pillars of the jurisprudence of the New Right: the reliance on original intentions, and the idea that the Constitution establishes a basically democratic or majoritarian scheme of government.

First, the jurisprudence of the Reagan administration is, according to Attorney General Meese, a Jurisprudence of Original Intent. The idea of referring to specific historical intentions as a way of closing the meaning of the general phrases actually written into the Constitution is extremely popular, but enormously problematic. As I've already indicated, the text of the Constitution sets moral and political, not historical questions for us. The Framers were capable of being specific when they wanted to be, so when they used general language we should take this as a deliberate delegation to future interpreters.

And the Framers' actions speak even louder than their words:

99

The Philadelphia convention was conducted in secret. And contrary to what Meese has said, the proceedings of the convention are *not* a matter of public record. What we have are the personal notes of several delegates; whose should we pick? Madison's are by far the most extensive, but Madison was a participant, not a neutral observer, and Madison waited half a century to publish his notes, publishing them after everyone else who had been at the convention was dead. We have no way of checking his accuracy.

If the Framers wanted future interpreters to be guided by their particular unstated intentions about individual rights, why did they keep the convention secret? Why did they write broad moral purposes into their statement of intentions in the preamble? Why did they write a Ninth Amendment which refers, not to historical entitlements, but to unspecified rights which people have prior to any constitutive act of government? If the Framers intended us to be guided by their specific intentions, they chose an idiotic strategy for communicating that intention to us.

Passing over these problems, the proponents of historical intent are still a long way from home: whose intent counts? The Framers' or the ratifiers'? Proponents of Original Intent always talk about the Framers, but the state ratifying conventions gave the Constitution the force of law; constructing a unified intent from hundreds of delegates to 13 state ratifying conventions will be a good trick if it can be brought off.

Another problem: what counts as *evidence* of intent? Only public records? Why not private correspondence?

And what happens when we find out the Framers disagreed about many things: that sometimes they chose general language because that was all they could agree upon?

At other times they chose general language as a deliberate delegation to future interpreters, including the courts. To substitute specific, unstated intentions for the general terms actually chosen is to disregard, not to respect, the framers and the Constitution.

100

But let's turn from this basket case of Original Intent to the second pillar of the New Right's jurisprudence: The claim that the Constitution establishes a "basically democratic" scheme of government, and thus that the Supreme Court's power is anomalous and must be carefully circumscribed. As Bork puts it: "The makers of our Constitution . . . provided wide powers to representative assemblies and ruled only a few subjects off limits by the Constitution."

This basically democratic rendering of the Constitution fits much contemporary ideology. It suits both the morally skeptical majoritarianism of the right, and the left-wing, democratic egalitarianism of Justice William Brennan.

But we need not be detained by the question of whose version of democracy is best, because the Constitution is not basically democratic. The Constitution checks and limits the popular will in a host of ways; it establishes a government of enumerated powers and broad individual rights of which the judiciary is an integral part.

Chaos and factional strife in the states led to the Constitutional Convention and to the rejection of democracy in favor of republican government. Mechanisms were adopted to check the popular will and to allow statesmen to stand against popular passions in favor of justice and the public good. Senators were originally chosen by state legislators; their terms are still long and each state still gets two regardless of population. Separated powers, checks and balances, and the embrace by one national government of a vast territory all make it difficult for a popular majority to gain effective control of the government. And a vital part of this scheme of institutional checks is an independent judiciary with coordinate status and life tenure. Nothing in the Constitution supports the call for judicial restraint. Justices take an oath to support the Constitution as supreme law, and their institutional design, "their permanent tenure," as Hamilton put it in the *Federalist,* no. 78, makes the courts "bulwarks of a limited Constitution against legislative encroachments."

Leaving procedural and institutional safeguards to one side, those who claim the Constitution establishes broad powers and few and narrow rights precisely reverse the logic of the Constitution itself: Congress's powers are enumerated and specific, individual rights are left broad and unspecified. This is why Hamilton argued, in the *Federalist*, no. 84, that "the Constitution is itself, in every rational sense, and to every useful purpose, a Bill of Rights." A Bill of Rights was eventually proposed and ratified, but the logic of enumerated powers and broad rights was preserved by the Ninth and Tenth Amendments, explicitly denying that individual rights are limited to those specified, and reserving all powers not delegated to the states and the people.

And so the Constitution establishes a scheme of government that is not basically democratic or majoritarian, but republican, whose powers are limited and which is charged with enforcing a broad array of individual rights. The judiciary is not an anomalous institution, but an integral part of a scheme of constitutionally limited government. Seen in this light, the Court is warranted in exercising its powers to the fullest.

If the Court, then, is fully justified on constitutional grounds in actively protecting individual rights against the government, it does not follow that any form of activism will do. The New Right is correct in charging the activists of the Warren Court with a failure of principle. While the Warren Court correctly perceived the Constitution's concern with racial equality and personal privacy, to take two examples, the liberal activists neglected the central place that the Constitution gives to economic liberties and property rights: In the contracts clause, the takings clause, and the Fourteenth Amendment's extension of the protection of due process of law to the life, liberty, and property of citizens in the states, the Constitution manifests a concern with economic liberties that conscientious interpreters cannot ignore.

A principled activism proposes that we see the Constitution as an attempt to realize the purposes disclosed by the document itself, its language, and structure: the protection of a broad array of rights, both personal and economic. A principled activism takes seriously the whole document, including those parts that liberal activists and the New Right ignore. We must accept the delegation implicit in the Framers' choice of general terms and not flee from the hard questions posed by the Constitution, either under the guise of respecting historical intentions or under the banner of a moral cynicism utterly inconsistent with the founding document and the project of the Framers. Indeed, the blanket moral cynicism of Bork and Rehnquist undermines any principled case for democracy itself, and so this cynicism proves self-defeating.

Besides the insistence on principle and fidelity to the text and structure of the Constitution itself, we have another way to control the judiciary.

We need to remember that the Court is only one of three coordinate branches, and each is charged with interpreting the Constitution for itself in carrying out its own duties. The Constitution is our supreme *political* document, to be interpreted not only by judges deciding cases but by all those who take an oath to support it, including members of Congress and the president. Attorney General Meese was absolutely right when he said, a few weeks ago, that Supreme Court interpretations of the Constitution are ultimate only for the judicial branch and not for coordinate branches of the federal government.

The Senate, in its recent hearings on the nominations of Chief Justice Rehnquist and Justice Antonin Scalia, missed an important opportunity to review the substantive merits of the jurisprudence of the New Right. In doing so, the Senate missed an opportunity to participate in the political process of constitutional interpretation. By confining itself to issues of intelligence and integrity, the Senate neglected its own responsibility to interpret and enforce the Constitution. Would substantive Senate oversight "politicize" the nomination process? It's already political. The president considers the substantive views of potential nominees, and the Senate should do the same before confirming.

Would substantive Senate review confound the president's appointment power? The president's power is to *nominate,* the power to *confirm* is the Senate's. And where the appointment in question is to a coordinate branch with life tenure, the president does not deserve the deference due to appointments within the executive branch, of which unity is a leading virtue. (In rejecting William Bradford Reynolds for a Justice Department position, but passing over the substantive views of Rehnquist and Scalia, the Senate reversed the proper levels of scrutiny.)

But will the open discussion and debate of the proper meaning of the Constitution further politicize the Court itself? And perhaps the Constitution? You bet it will, and high time too: because to do so would elevate our politics. Public debate about the meaning of the Constitution educates the public in its requirements, invites the public to pass on the interpretations of particular senators as elections occur, and helps make constitutional values a lively force in our politics. To politicize the Constitution in this way is to constitutionalize our politics: to elevate our politics above the pursuit of narrow interests and help give us a politics of principle.

Now of course this already happens to some degree, and the public is aware of the propriety of serious constitutional reflection in our politics. Take the recent case of Senator Slade Gorton, who, for political favors from the White House, traded his vote on the appointment of Daniel Manion to the federal bench. The people of Washington State, to their eternal credit, rewarded this bit of political corruption (utterly inappropriate to what the Framers hoped for in the Senate) with a justly deserved one-way ticket home for Senator Gorton.

To take up the active enforcement of constitutional principles in the courtroom and in the political arena broadly does not mean we will find easy answers to the hard questions of political morality posed by the Constitution. The Constitution is not easy to interpret. The important point is that the hard questions posed by principled activism are the right questions, the questions we ought to be asking not just in the courtroom but in our politics more broadly. The questions posed by the Jurisprudence of Original Intent on the other hand are not only impossible to answer but the wrong questions, questions that fly in the face of the moral seriousness of the founding document and its Framers.

Gary L. McDowell: Stephen Macedo's work is considered by many to be a brilliant effort in legal theory. My problem is that I distrust brilliant theories—perhaps for reasons personal as well as professional. I am not here to dispute the brilliance of his efforts but only to suggest we should be wary of such insightful things.

For in reading Mr. Macedo's book, and in listening to his presentation just now, I am reminded of the problem one confronts in making any argument. And that problem, to borrow the words of Benjamin Cardozo, is the tendency of an idea to exceed the limits of its logic.

In thinking about Mr. Macedo's argument, I was reminded of that great legal philosopher, Woody Allen. Allen, you might remember, is fascinated by logic, and in particular the problem of false steps. His famous example of syllogistic reasoning will, I think, make my point:

Major Premise: All men have legs

Minor Premise: Socrates has legs

Conclusion: All men are Socrates.

This is the sort of feeling I get when I hear or read Mr. Macedo's criticism of what he has erroneously dubbed the New Right's jurisprudence. For his attack on what has come to be called a Jurisprudence of Original Intention is an attack that begins from a fundamentally flawed understanding of what a Jurisprudence of Original Intention is really all about.

In particular, Mr. Macedo asserts that a Jurisprudence of Original Intention derives from two basic assumptions, assumptions with which he obviously disagrees. The first assumption is that to speak of the intentions of the Framers, one can only mean

105

what Macedo labels their "specific historical intentions." The second, and equally flawed, assumption attributed to a Jurisprudence of Original Intention is that it is little more than a cloak for a "political preference for majoritarian power over individual rights and liberty."

I suspect I will surprise no one by suggesting that Mr. Macedo is tragically wrong on both counts. But his misreading, not only of contemporary writers but of the Founders themselves, is so great that it cannot but be intended. The reason Mr. Macedo begins as he does is because his true interest is in pressing a particular political preference of his own disguised as disinterested scholarship.

To put it simply, Mr. Macedo's work is a classic example of the moral wish being father to the constitutional thought.

Let me turn first to the problem of his points of jurisprudential departure before turning to the problems posed by his point of ideological arrival.

First, as far as I know, no one who argues for a Jurisprudence of Original Intention—certainly not Attorney General Meese, whom Mr. Macedo takes to task—has ever suggested that this view is tied to the particular historical circumstances of the founding period. What is meant by "intention" is not particular or subjective notions of that time concerning public policy or law. Rather, what is meant is what Paul Bator has called the "postulates of good government." Those postulates differ from particular policy ends in that they rely most heavily on the structural design of a government, the means a government has of effecting certain policies. Toward that end, for example, it does not matter what James Madison or Alexander Hamilton or anyone else of that generation felt about, say, abortion as a moral matter. What does matter is whether such questions as abortion are properly handled by the federal judiciary or are appropriately left to the legislatures of the several states as a result of the Constitution's principle of federalism.

Thus, what lies behind a Jurisprudence of Original Intention is not a social agenda but a due regard for the Constitution's structure—from its enumeration of both powers and limits to its principles such as separation of powers and federalism. For taken as a whole, these particulars comprise the basic theory of the Constitution: limited but energetic government, with the power to act and a structure designed to make it act wisely or at least responsibly.

This leads directly to Mr. Macedo's second mistaken assumption. He believes that those who embrace this approach to constitutional affairs are basically nothing more than rather clumsy defenders of a crudely understood majoritarianism. To argue, as he does, that the security of our most important rights depends upon the judiciary engaging in moral philosophy in order to curb the excesses of an apparently indecent (in his view) process of majority rule, is to deny or at least ignore the rich and sophisticated theory of the American Founding, what Alexander Hamilton referred to as the newly bolstered science of politics.

In fact, the very substantive concerns Mr. Macedo raises were raised many times by the Founders. The problems of property being taken, of unjust tax laws, of the rights of any minority however defined—economic, religious, ethnic, or otherwise—being abused by a zealous and overbearing majority, were precisely the issues that drove the delegates to Philadelphia in 1787. These were precisely the concerns the Constitution was meant to address and remedy. One need only read the *Federalist*, no. 10, to understand this. Thus, it seems, Mr. Macedo and I agree on the problems to be expected under a majoritarian scheme. But we differ markedly on the means appropriate to secure those ends.

The fact of the matter is that the Founders sought to create a system of government which would not deny the will of the majority but which would, as Madison so tellingly put it, refine and enlarge it. Thus, they, too, feared the excesses of democracy and the tyranny of the majority. But what they sought was a system whereby the crude and untutored opinions and passions and interests of the people would be filtered and thus refined and improved upon. What they sought, in brief, was not a simple *quantitative* majoritarianism but a *qualitative* majoritarianism.

This was to be achieved through the carefully drawn structural contrivances of the Constitution—and not upon any one institutional part of it. It would have struck that generation as bizarre to have expected the security of their rights to depend upon a judiciary willing to plunge into a moral discourse unattached to the text and divorced from the intentions that lie behind the document itself. Indeed, one need only read the *Federalist*, no. 78 or *Marbury* v. *Madison* (1803) to see the limited role they anticipated for the courts under the Constitution.

Thus the true foundation of a jurisprudence of original intention is the appreciation for the design and the objects of the Constitution. It recognizes the limitations of popular government and the need to secure individual rights—both personal and economic. But it denies that good government is ever to be expected in an unelected body of nine (give or take what Congress may see fit to change that number to) so overwhelmed with the pursuit of moral progress that they become willing, as Chancellor Kent once put it, to "roam at large in the tractless fields of their own imaginations."

Indeed, our constitutional institutions were devised precisely to supply, as Madison said in the *Federalist*, no. 51, "the defect of better motives." Sturdy institutions replaced good intentions as the source of good government.

Now I would like to turn to Mr. Macedo's more substantive concerns. That is, those objects he would both hope and expect to have judges reach once they start meandering down the moral path he has cleared for them.

His concern is twofold: economic rights on the one hand, and personal rights on the other. His means of achieving a jurisprudence dedicated to both is the same. It is, to put it bluntly, to allow judges to play fast and loose with the Constitution.

To put it briefly, Mr. Macedo's logic is guided by reference to two of constitutional decisional law's strangest polestars— *Lochner* v. *New York* (1905) and *Griswold* v. *Connecticut* (1965). These are, of course, the two exemplars of substantive due process, old and new. In each case, the Court looked beyond the text of the Constitution, beyond the intention of those who framed and ratified the Fourteenth Amendment, and beyond the limits of common constitutional sense.

The liberty of contract doctrine of *Lochner* and the right to privacy doctrine of *Griswold* are ultimately rooted in the same shallow soil, that of personal predilection and political preference. They are juridical contrivances at war with the Constitution, at war with the idea of limited government, and at war with the basic principles of democratic government upon which our entire political system and legal traditions rest.

Where the Constitution intends to protect rights, it does so— clearly and simply. Where it is silent, it is silent. The due process clause is not a judicial wild card to be used to smuggle moral theory into the Constitution; the Ninth Amendment is not a statement of fundamental rights so sweeping as to render all the other rights explicitly mentioned superfluous; most of all, Article III is not the primary means whereby rights are to find their primary protection.

Mr. Macedo's theory, if taken seriously, would render the Supreme Court not so much a continuing constitutional convention but a wildly esoteric Ivy League seminar in moral philosophy.

Thus, the notions of substantive due process that lie at the root of Mr. Macedo's theory are notions that should be rejected. The due process clauses, after all, were meant to secure those rather technical procedures all are rightfully due as part of the judicial process, as Alexander Hamilton once had occasion to explain. Those clauses were never intended to empower the judicial branch to inquire into the substance of legislation at either the state or the national level to determine if such legislation is reasonable or nonarbitrary or whatever. The reason, as James Wilson put it during the Federal Convention, is that some laws may be unwise, they may be dangerous, they may be destructive—but still not be unconstitutional. To allow the courts to enter the realm of substantive policymaking is to deny the logic and the limits of the written Constitution that still governs us.

To distrust the moral impulses of judges is not to be morally cynical. It is, rather, to be politically prudent.

With all this being said, there is a deeper danger to Mr. Macedo's book. As I have said in another place, this joining of the traditions of *Lochner* and *Griswold* is a most unholy coupling of the liberal left and the libertarian right. The offspring of this curious union can only be the bastard child of judicial activism.

Both efforts call into question in a most radical way the constitutional structures that grant legitimacy to the popular branches of the government. Each side rejects any confidence in the power of legislatures to govern decently, and each has a greater confidence in the legal argument of advocates than in the political opinions of the people duly expressed in properly representative institutions.

In the end, this aconstitutional jurisprudence of the liberal left and the libertarian right will weaken public confidence in the Constitution's institutional design that has for so long made this nation not only the most free the world has known, but the most economically prosperous.

In closing, let me briefly return to the problem of brilliance in legal theory and read a portion of a recent article in the *New Republic*. No one has said it better as regards the contemporary confusion surrounding the Fourteenth Amendment.

[Ronald] Dworkin's theory, like [John Hart] Ely's, takes the constitutional text as the starting point, but then adds a brilliant gloss of its own.

Unfortunately, these theories share a flaw, a flaw endemic to brilliant legal theories. The 14th Amendment was not written by Ronald Dworkin or John Hart Ely. Its primary drafter was a man named John Bingham. Bingham had a certain flair for sermonizing. But, based on his public speeches, it seems doubtful that he was as intelligent as the average law professor, let alone Ronald Dworkin or John Hart Ely. It is hard to see how he could have had in mind a notion so ingenious that no one thought of it until Ronald Dworkin and John Hart Ely came along.

Not everyone agrees that the intent of the framers is what counts in constitutional interpretation. But virtually everyone agrees that a bedrock principle of law is consent of the governed. A brilliant theory is by definition one that would not occur to most people. The general problem with brilliant legal theories is: How can most people have agreed to something that they could not conceive of?

Justice Hugo Black once said that judges and justices take an oath to support the Constitution as it is, not as they would like it to be. The same should be required of scholarship. We should endeavor to understand and to teach and write about the Constitution as it is, not as we would like it to be.

Macedo: Let me turn first to Gary's ironic emphasis on the "brilliance" of my argument. The real irony is this: Gary thinks, no doubt, that he has an even more brilliant argument to show that mine is not the best interpretation of the Constitution, so his criticisms turn back on themselves, at least if he thinks his arguments are better than mine.

Indeed, Gary's criticisms turn back on the Reagan administration itself. This administration has encouraged the academic study of the Constitution by promoting so many professors to the federal bench and to important positions in the Justice Department: Justice Scalia and Judges Bork, Posner, Easterbrook, and Winter were all well-known academics. Gary McDowell and even the attorney general are former professors. And it seems to me that all these former professors are capable of articulating theories of the Constitution that are not only, as Gary would have it, "brilliant," but sometimes utterly fantastic.

Gary closed by warning that we should beware of brilliant academic theories that would never occur to practicing politicians or common people, theories that the people could not understand as interpretations of the Constitution. I agree. But the American people and those who framed the Constitution would have no difficulty grasping the idea that they have rights, both personal and economic, and that these rights are guaranteed by the Constitution. I suspect they would find the contrary notion, expressed by Chief Justice Rehnquist and Judge Bork, that rights claims are reducible to mere preferences or desires for gratification, extremely difficult to grasp.

Now Gary seemed, at least initially, to concede that he rejects the relevance of specific historical intentions to the project of constitutional interpretation. He conceded that the Constitution is not basically democratic or majoritarian, and he claimed that he's not really a moral skeptic. But in condemning the interpretive style of *Griswold* v. *Connecticut*, it seems to me that Gary must rely upon the sorts of claims he says he wants to eschew. Any conscientious constitutionalist must be prepared to allow the judicial protection of rights not explicitly stated in the founding document, and that is because the founding document itself tells us, in the Ninth Amendment, that we have such rights. How else can we interpret the Ninth Amendment except by engaging in the project of *Griswold?*

What *Griswold* does is to flesh out those unspecified constitutional rights by looking for principles and values implicit in the rights that are specified. And so we find that the Third Amendment protects the privacy of the home against the quartering of troops, the Fourth protects persons and their homes against unreasonable searches and seizures, the Fifth protects persons against self-incrimination, and First Amendment guarantees have been interpreted to imply a right to free association. A principle of respect for the privacy of individuals would explain and justify

112

the inclusion of these specific guarantees in the Constitution. This implicit principle is, then, an appropriate basis for filling out the other, unspecified constitutional rights that the Ninth Amendment tells us we have. This is a principled, textual way of justifying the right to privacy extended to the intimate relations of married couples in *Griswold*, and which should have been extended to homosexuals in the recent case of *Bowers v. Hardwick*.

The method of *Griswold* for giving substance to unspecified constitutional rights is, incidentally, the same logic that Chief Justice Marshall applied to Congress's powers in the landmark case of *McCulloch v. Maryland*. Article 2 enumerates Congress's powers and then adds that Congress may also do what is "necessary and proper" to carry out the enumerated powers. But what other powers are "necessary and proper"? Marshall sought to discern the objects and ends underlying and justifying the enumerated powers. Additional powers might, then, be justified as means to the objects and ends implicit in specific grants of power. If we cannot justify the logic of *Griswold*, then we cannot justify the logic of *McCulloch*: the one seeks a principled, textual basis for the unspecified powers announced by the necessary and proper clause, the other seeks a similar basis for unspecified rights whose existence is even more clearly announced by the Ninth Amendment.

Gary also seems to claim that the Fourteenth Amendment's guarantees of "due process of law," equal protection, and so on do not warrant judicial forays into moral and philosophical questions. He mentions the Court's controversial abortion decision, *Roe v. Wade*, as an example of misconceived judicial activism. Well, how can judges enforce the Fourteenth Amendment's guarantee of the equal protection of the law for all persons without deciding what counts as a person worthy of constitutional protection? We may disagree with the particular answer the Court announced in *Roe*, but surely the Court cannot avoid the issue.

But Gary also claims the principle of federalism ought to preclude judicial inquiry into "such questions as abortion." Does

Gary seriously mean that judges should leave the protection of individual rights to the states? Does he need to be reminded of the Civil War and the sweeping amendments passed after that war guaranteeing fundamental rights against state governments? Does he regard civil rights decisions like *Brown* v. *Board of Education* as illegitimate judicial infringements on "states' rights"?

Gary's case against a principled judicial activism rests, ultimately, on the claim that constitutional "structures"—the separation of powers and federalism—and not the judiciary are the basic guarantees of limited government and individual rights. In this, Gary wrongly supposes that the Framers pursued a simple, rather than a complex and multifaceted, strategy for limiting government and protecting individual rights. Of course the Framers hoped that separated powers, a bicameral legislature, long terms for senators, the embrace by one government of a large, heterogeneous republic, and other structural measures would help prevent factions from passing unjust laws. This in no way implies, however, that the judiciary was expected to exercise restraint in striking down whatever unjust laws do manage to pass. And for Gary to cite the *Federalist*, no. 78, to support the claim that the Framers envisioned a "limited role" for the Court is ludicrous. The *Federalist*, no. 78, argues for granting life tenure to Supreme Court justices so that they will have the "uncommon portion of fortitude" needed to guard the Constitution against legislative encroachments. Without the courts, according to the *Federalist*, no. 78, the limits on legislative power expressed in the Constitution would amount to nothing, and so the courts are to be "bulwarks of a limited Constitution." I cannot imagine a less plausible source of support for Gary's position than the *Federalist*, no. 78, unless perhaps it would be the Constitution itself.

The Constitution's structure has been changed in important ways since the founding. In the original design, not only the Court but the president and the Senate were remote from the people and were expected to have the good judgment needed to support minority rights against popular passions. As a consequence, we should hardly be surprised if the modern Court has become more active in defending constitutional limits than the Framers anticipated: the courts are defending these limits against institutions markedly more popular than in the original design.

Let me just say in closing that the courts should not flee from the hard moral judgments posed by the Constitution, as Gary McDowell and the New Right would have them do. Of course, the judges cannot protect rights by themselves: that is an argument for greater legislative responsibility, that is a good argument for more serious legislative consideration of constitutional issues; it is no argument at all for judicial restraint in the protection of minority rights.

About the Author

Stephen Macedo, an assistant professor in the Government Department at Harvard University, is the author of *Liberal Virtues: A Liberal Theory of Citizenship, Virtue, and Community*, forthcoming from Oxford University Press. He holds degrees from the London School of Economics, Oxford University, and Princeton University, and is an adjunct scholar of the Cato Institute.

Cato Institute

Founded in 1977, the Cato Institute is a public policy research foundation dedicated to broadening the parameters of policy debate to allow consideration of more options that are consistent with the traditional American principles of limited government, individual liberty, and peace. Toward that goal, the Institute strives to achieve a greater involvement of the intelligent, concerned lay public in questions of policy and the proper role of government.

The Institute is named for *Cato's Letters*, pamphlets that were widely read in the American Colonies in the early eighteenth century and played a major role in laying the philosophical foundation for the revolution that followed. Since that revolution, civil and economic liberties have been eroded as the number and complexity of social problems have grown. Today virtually no aspect of human life is free from the domination of a governing class of politico-economic interests. A pervasive intolerance for individual rights is shown by government's arbitrary intrusions into private economic transactions and its disregard for civil liberties.

To counter this trend the Cato Institute undertakes an extensive publications program dealing with the complete spectrum of policy issues. Books, monographs, and shorter studies are commissioned to examine the federal budget, Social Security, regulation, NATO, international trade, and a myriad of other issues. Major policy conferences are held throughout the year, from which papers are published thrice yearly in the *Cato Journal*.

In order to maintain an independent posture, the Cato Institute accepts no government funding. Contributions are received from foundations, corporations, and individuals, and other revenue is generated from the sale of publications. The Institute is a nonprofit, tax-exempt, educational foundation under Section 501(c)3 of the Internal Revenue Code.

CATO INSTITUTE
224 Second St., S.E.
Washington, D.C. 20003